9 Myths About Muslim Charities

STORIES FROM THE ZAKAT FOUNDATION OF AMERICA

D1478236

9 Myths About Muslim Charities

Stories from the Zakat Foundation of America

Halil I. Demir

Zakat Foundation of America

Zakat Foundation of America
7421 W 100th Pl, Bridgeview, IL 60455
United States of America
tel: 708.233.0555 fax: 708.233.0339 toll-free: 1.888.925.2887
website: zakat.org
Email: info@zakat.org

This book is printed on premium acid-free paper that meets the minimum requirements for alkaline papers by the American National Standard for Information Sciences — Permanence of paper for printed Library Materials ANSI Z39.48-1984.

This typeface facilitates Arabic transliteration and the use of features special to writing on Islam, such as "ﷺ" and "ﷻ".

Translated citations of The Quran in this book are from *The Gracious Quran: A Modern-Phrased Interpretation in English* by Ahmad Zaki Hammad with occasional modification. Bible citations are from the NRSV.

Although every precaution has been taken to verify the accuracy of the information contained herein, the author and publisher assume no responsibility for any errors or omissions. No liability is assumed for damages that may result from the use of information contained within.

Cover Design: Walaa T. Khalaf

Printed in the United States of America

ISBN: 978-1-7339688-0-5 (hardcover) — 978-1-7339688-1-2 (softcover) — 978-1-7339688-2-9 (eBook)

LCCN: 2019904624

First Edition

10 9 8 7 6 5 4 3 2 1   25 24 23 22 21 20 19

For America's Muslims

Unheralded in Selfless Giving

Undaunted Before Withering Aspersion

*Unfailing in Zakat-Alms & Bearing Witness to All
with Charity*

Let the World Know Their Story

PRESIDENT FRANKLIN DELANO ROOSEVELT
An Excerpt from His Annual Message to Congress
January 6, 1941

"In the future days, which we seek to make secure, we look forward to a world founded upon four essential human freedoms:

The first is **freedom of speech and expression** — everywhere in the world.

The second is **freedom of every person to worship God in his own way** — everywhere in the world.

The third is **freedom from want** — which, translated into universal terms, means economic understandings which will secure to every nation a healthy peacetime life for its inhabitants — everywhere in the world.

The fourth is **freedom from fear** — which, translated into world terms, means a worldwide reduction of armaments to such a point and in such a thorough fashion that no nation will be in a position to commit an act of physical aggression against any neighbor — anywhere in the world.

That is no vision of a distant millennium. It is a definite basis for a kind of world attainable in our own time and generation."

TRANSLITERATION NOTE

The transliteration of Arabic names and terms into English follows a well-established scheme, shown below. Nearly every mention of the name of the Prophet Muhammad ﷺ is followed by the Arabic calligraphic symbol "ﷺ," translated as God bless him and grant him peace. The Arabic prayer "عليه السلام," peace be upon him, appears after the names of other prophets and the Arch-Angel Gabriel عليه السلام. The Arabic calligraphic prayer symbol "عليها السلام" follows the name of Mary عليها السلام, mother of Jesus عليه السلام.

ء .... '	ج .... z	ك .... k
ا .... â or a	س .... s	ل l
ب .... b	ش ......sh	م .... m
ت .... t	ص .... ṣ	ن .... n
ث .... th	ض ...... ḍ	ه .... h
ج .... j	ط .... ṭ	و .... û or u w (consonant)
ح .... ḥ	ظ .... ẓ	
خ .... kh	ع .... '	ي ......î or i or iyy y (consonant)
د .... d	غ ...... gh	ة .... t (ending)
ذ .... dh	ف .... f	
ر .... r	ق .... q	

QURAN CITATION NOTE

The translated text of verses of the Quran and the Bible appear in the color maroon, with the Quran's verses between decorative parentheses, also in maroon "❖." References to the verses of the Quran are cited in standard parentheses as "Sûrah" Name (Quran chapter); "Comma"; Sûrah "Number"; "Colon"; Verse "Number." For example, the third verse of the Quran's first *sûrah* is cited as (Sûrat Al-Fâtiḥah, 1:3).

CONTENTS

WHAT IS THE ZAKAT FOUNDATION?
A PARABLE

OFTEN, I AM asked the question that titles this Foreword. I think a story answers best.

The Baker and the Man in Need

There once was a baker, the best in all Anatolia. One day he said to himself, "Today, I will bake a bread so fine, it will be perfect, the perfect loaf of bread. And I will give it to the most perfect one I know."

He set himself to making a surpassing dough from the very best flour and yeast. He kneaded and watered, and squeezed and patted to perfection. Then he covered it with a splendid cloth in ideal warmth for just the right time, while he kindled and stoked his stone and clay oven with wonderful wood to the precise temperature. He lovingly formed the dough into a flawless loaf, covered it to rise again, then placed it on his wooden peel and slid it with care to the exact center of the oven. At just the right moment, he removed the loaf, golden pure. He had baked the perfect loaf of bread.

"Who, now, shall I give it to? Someone perfect."

Try as he might, the baker could think of no one worthy of his perfected labor. "None is perfect, none but the One who fashioned with His Hands the Heavens and Earth, and all things in them. I shall give it to the Only Worthy. I shall gift it to God."

With that the baker wrapped his work, undid his apron, donned his mantle, and headed to the Blue Mosque. He entered, carefully placed his bread loaf on the pulpit, and offered his prayer of greeting, bowing his face down to the ground in obeisance.

When he finished, the baker sat on his knees and raised his open hands to the Heavens. He began to weep.

"O God! You have created me, and all the worlds, and all that flies through the air, burrows in the soil, and walks and crawls between them. You alone are perfect and create with perfection. You have honored me, taught me to bake, fed me, clothed me, sheltered me, and enriched me and all my family from it. So I have made the perfect loaf and I offer it to You, O God. You, You alone accept the sincere and best offering. Please accept it from me, my Lord, and make it a cause of blessing for me with You."

With that, the baker stood up, dried his eyes, and headed back to his bakery.

He didn't see the man who entered the Blue Mosque just after him. Neither did the man see him leave. The man left his worn shoes at the entranceway, offered his greeting prayer near the pulpit, finished and began to weep.

"O God! I have left my family hungry and in need and have come to this city in search of Your bounty, through toil and diligence. You know I am a hard worker, my Lord. You know my straitened condition. And you know, my Lord, I cannot bring myself to ask provision from another, when You, You alone are the Giver of Provision, Creator of all things. O Originator of the Heavens and all that is in them! O Fashioner of the Earth and all that its skies uphold, its clay enfolds, and its waters bear, I have searched out Your provision for days with no morsel, and I am hungry, penniless, and have come unto You, in Whom none is let down. Save me. Enrich me. Feed me. Preserve my dignity, O You Who are the

All-Rich, the Loving-Kind, the All-Giving, O God."

With that very last breath, his streaming eyes lit upon the perfect loaf, perched on the pulpit. The wonder-struck man leaped to his feet and cradled the bread in his still outstretched palms. It was the most perfect loaf of bread he had ever seen.

With joy his heart burst and the words broke from his lips. "O my Lord! Ever did I know Your generosity, Your care for the least of Your creatures, that You are the Answerer of Prayers. But never did I know with what speed and haste You aid and comfort Your needful servants, my Lord."

How grateful I am, my Lord, ever grateful and at Your service. You, the Lord of All of the Worlds, King and Lord of the Magnificent Throne, You grant so majestic a gift to so meek a man as me? In thankful gratitude to You, You alone, my Lord, every day shall I strive in Your way. And every day shall I do for Your needful servants, like me, the best that my hands will have done, for so long as You give me breath and strength and a knowing heart. You are the One."

With that, he fell to the chin, weeping praise and thanks. He arose and left renewed with the bread, fed by his Lord.

At that moment, walking back to his shop, a burning thought pierced the baker's heart. "Will my Lord accept my offering, humble a man as I am? How shall I know?" In one motion, he turned back upon his steps to the Blue Mosque, filled with the need to know if God had blessed his gift. In no time, he had entered the mosque. His mouth fell open, speechless. His perfect loaf was gone.

At once, his heart pumped and jumped. Delight swelled in his chest. "O my Lord!" he said. "Ever did I know Your generosity, Your care for the least of Your creatures, that You are the Answerer of Prayers. But never did I know with what speed and haste You accept and receive the good deeds of Your sincere servants, my Lord.

How grateful I am, my Lord, ever grateful and at Your service. You, the Lord of All of the Worlds, King and Lord of the Magnificent Throne, You accept so plain a gift from so meek a man as me? In thankful gratitude to You, You alone, my Lord, every day shall I bake. And every day shall I bring to You the best that my hands have done, for so long as You give me breath and strength and a knowing heart. You are the One."

With that, he fell to the chin, weeping praise and thanks. He rose and left renewed with his gift, favored by his Lord.

The Soul of the Zakat Foundation

The Zakat Foundation of America, in essence, is *that* plea, that earnest supplication, that urgent entreaty, both of the baker and the man in need. We are the prayer between the sincere giver, to whom God has granted resources, and the needful receiver, whom circumstances beyond the person have elevated to the central moral test of our time, our societies, and the human worth of the rest of us.

Servanthood is the embodiment of this prayer, and, therefore, a worldly station of honor. It is the condition for which the people who direct, staff, and uphold the Zakat Foundation strive, however imperfectly. We serve our Creator by serving His servants. Our source of focus and field of vision are no less specific and encompassing, respectively, than the perspective that these two points of orientation frame, which are literally Heaven and earth. Such is the state I aspire to live in, a builder for the benevolent who dream of a better world for the near and the far neighbor to live as one. Serving our givers. Serving our receivers. Serving our Zakat Foundation workers and volunteers — all in the service of my Lord, all at His pleasure.

That is the Zakat Foundation ethos (mingled with my own). But there is something more germane still to be said about founding and guiding an American Muslim charity that began its life only weeks before 9/11 with just one part-time employee and a few volunteers; that has come these 207 months since through relentless, ubiquitous vitriol propagated against Islam and Muslims, which persist with even more threat and ferocity in these latter days of 2018; and that our donors, volunteers, staff, and leadership have now built, with the blessing of God, into a worldwide American Muslim charity with passionate personnel, welcoming offices, life-saving projects, and diverse partners on five continents …

… Which brings us to the intent of this little book: to convey to you what likely only someone at the helm of a global American Muslim charity could about the humanitarian conditions of our world and the condition of the humanitarian impulse among us here at home.

Charity and the American Muslim Predicament

I began by telling you the parable of the Zakat Foundation. In the course of this book, I will relate nine more stories to you, not metaphorical tales but true accounts that illustrate the formidable gauntlet of skepticism we at Zakat Foundation (and most every Muslim charity in America) are continually compelled to run just to make it possible for American Muslims to help people, including American Christians, Jews, and others in dire need who are not Muslim.

Our predicament is yet graver than this. Islam obligates its adherents, if they would be faithful ones, to bear witness to the belief they claim for their hearts in two financial ways:

First, Muslims must give in alms 2.5 percent of the wealth they accumulate in a year beyond their needs and obligations. This is Zakat, the Third of the celebrated Five Pillars of Islam (from which the Zakat Foundation of America takes its name). Properly speaking, Zakat is no "gift" to the poor or tax on the rich. It is a one-year bond yield paid from the Divine Treasury into the accounts of people on behalf of the needful and due them in full at maturity. Plainly put, Zakat is not a mandated charity to be annually "given up." Rather, the sole and rightful beneficiaries of 2.5 percent of every individual's excess yearly wealth are not oneself, but those in need around one. Default on this pivotal payment to the poor is a major sin. Rejection of Zakat and its remittance puts one outside the fold of Islam.

Second, Muslims owe a charitable action every day for each of the 360 articulating junctures of the human skeleton. The Prophet Muhammad ﷺ said: "Every day the sun rises, people are indebted for every joint of their body and are to perform a charitable deed for each one" (Al-Nawawi, *Forty Hadiths*, No. 26).

So the humanitarian stakes spiral high for the conscientious Muslim. One is compelled to vindicate his or her faith with both mandatory and freewill charitable outlays that lift human suffering and burden. On top of this, one is to steward all other earthly existence besides — plant and animal, earth, sky, and water — for the Quran (the Muslim scripture, which Muslims take with utmost seriousness in religion) holds humankind accountable for this benevolence, as well.

⤛⤜

Zakat Foundation of America – What '*of*' Really Means

Here, then, is my testimony set forthrightly before you. My purpose is your friendship and support for Zakat Foundation for what we do in the world.

We seek not merely to aid but to *enrich* the poor. We feed the hungry, yes. But we teach them techniques and equip them also for food-resilient farming and connect them to the market to profit. We act to slake the thirst of the parched. Then we plan with the thirsty and work alongside them to engineer self-sustaining water sources, pure and in abundance, for their communities.

We shelter the refugee, then deliver the family intact to resettlement, retraining, new-language literacy, education, and earning through trade and jobs. We stand by the widow and the single mother and do not desert her, but support her through to self-reliance with skills-acquisition courses that ready her for employment, or more desirably to empowered entrepreneurship. We foster the orphan in safety to an educated maturity and independence.

We rebuild houses that reclaim the family lives of the bombed-out homeless, stripped of everything, including their pride and will to thrive. We restore livelihoods to the displaced destitute foraging food in grasslands, and restart ruined lives in remote villages, with a gift of mating dairy pairs and animal husbandry training.

We underwrite anti-gun violence initiatives in city neighborhoods and send those local school children with packs full of supplies back into classrooms. We distribute holiday foods to struggling families and toys to their children. We hand-deliver medical aid, nursing services, hygiene and winter kits, bedding and heaters, cooking and household utensils, emergency food and water, and prepaid debit cards to people hit by disaster in America and abroad.

What we *never* do is ask our beneficiaries about their race, ethnicity, or religious beliefs. We judge not their behaviors nor attribute their affliction to the judgment of God. We attach no strings, make no demands, permit no *quid pro quo* in exchange for the gifts our donors give freely and our workers offer humbly to our desperate and vulnerable neighbors at home or across the world. We seek only the Face of God.

What if not the very best of the American tradition do these Zakat Foundation relief policies show us? We are a homegrown American Muslim charity. Our humanitarian work embodies the highest standard of American values. It spreads the generosity of our American supporters to the places and people most direly in need of it on earth. As such,

Zakat Foundation represents the best of America, an expression of its citizenry's humanity we ought to extol and uphold.

Yet a pall of mistrust, thick with bad information and frightful intimations, hangs over Muslims and Islam in these times. This veil has emerged as the most dangerous threat to America's democratic vision and societal principles of republicanism since perhaps the Civil War. It obscures (and is meant to) the good will and dignified humanity in the hearts of millions who grow wary of one another in the dark.

I have seen firsthand a thousand and one times how the mere mental association of an American relief organization with Islam blinds otherwise clear-sighted people to the most obvious truths and simplest good deeds. Awareness that we are a "Muslim" humanitarian agency suddenly short-circuits their capacity to make a connection between the Zakat Foundation and the urgency of the life-saving support and compassionate care our people consistently deliver, at enormous personal sacrifice and risk, to hundreds of thousands at the reaches of the earth in the desolate hour of their need.

So there our recipients wait, suffering at the edge of hope, thinking all is lost, deeming themselves abandoned … until God shall deliver them our relief. The delays in aid for some prove too late.

When I began this book, the people of Eastern Ghouta on the outskirts of Damascus huddled in basements and rubble — malnourished, dehydrated, wounded, and scared — trapped beneath an evil rain. Three of our relief workers had just died there pulling women and children from the rubble of barrel-bombed basements. They were there to enroll children with parents killed in the war in our Orphan Sponsorship Program.

As I write these final words, the relentless bombing of Yemen has crossed into its fifth year on March 26, 2019. The UN World Food Program (WFP) stated: "Today 20 million Yemenis – some 70 percent of the population – are food insecure, marking a 13 percent increase from last year." Almost 10 million of these noncombatants "are one step away from famine." The World Health Organization (WHO) documented more than 1 million cholera cases in 2017, a third under age 5. This preventable scourge has returned, WHO recording 108,889 suspected cholera cases from January 1 to March 17, 2019.

Yemen remains the world's largest humanitarian crisis. Yet charities have scant access to feed, clothe, shelter, and heal these innocents because of a tacitly sanctioned siege. Moreover, government agencies and banks have quietly colluded to mire relief organizations like Zakat Foundation in a morass of unwritten rules that opaquely prevent our transparent execution of universally recognized, sound humanitarian practices. For example, Bank of America and BMO management suddenly ordered their local branches to unilaterally "de-risk" and close our accounts in the summer of 2017, on the pretext of regularly scheduled payments we had been sending (to great praise) for years to support the education of rural university students in Afghanistan.

Suspicion, paranoia even, and sometimes an underlying ill will have been drilled into the American psyche by a growing public curriculum of fear and dehumanization that relentlessly defames Islam and vilifies Muslims. These morph into monstrous obstacles to Zakat Foundation's relief work and become obstructions that loom even larger than the impediments of the wars, droughts, earthquakes, and hurricanes we face.

An Invitation to Humanity

This is the ever more rocky and risky humanitarian terrain Zakat Foundation and other American Muslim charities now negotiate. With this landscape before your mind's eye, and with the heart to shepherd America through troubled times to its highest promise, hear my plea. I appeal to the earnestness of your soul. Meet us. Know us. Accompany us. Witness our work. Then together let us heed President Abraham Lincoln's 1858 warning to America that rings out like an omen of prescience today: "A house divided against itself cannot stand."

Let us tear down these mounting walls of shadow and distrust that would rend apart our society. Let the loving light of good-hearted people just like you break through. Let the charity they send pierce the gloom of those who but for the grace of God could be you. Let its relief reach the aching wounded, touch the bereaved powerless, settle the dislocated and destitute.

Millions of lives depend on it … nearly as much as our own moral survival as a nation and as human beings.

Halil I. Demir
Bridgeview, Illinois
May 2019

AMERICAN MUSLIM CHARITIES
ARE TREATED LIKE OTHER CHARITIES

WHEN JESUS SAW the crowds, he went up the mountain; and after he sat down, his disciples came to him: Then he began to speak, and taught them, saying:

" … Blessed are you, when people revile you and persecute you and utter all kinds of evil against you falsely, on my account. Rejoice and be glad, for your reward is great in Heaven, for in the same way they persecuted the prophets who were before you."

(New Revised Standard Version, Matt. 5.1-2, 11-12)

The Transfer

It's early Friday morning, September 22, 2006. I get a phone call from our bank saying I must come in immediately. The bank has said it cannot execute a crucial wire transfer I've sent to help Afghan refugees in Pakistan.

I'm hoping to clear this up quickly. Local food suppliers need to get paid before our people can distribute the provisions among a desperate population. Because it's Friday, and I need to make the congregational prayer by 1 p.m.

I'm at the bank by 9:15 a.m. A bank officer who knows me ushers me into her office and sits me down. I ask her about the transfer problem.

"Well, Mr. Demir, our bank cannot make the transfer because Pakistan is not a country."

I'm momentarily stunned into silence. Is she giving me an early morning ribbing to lighten things up? No laugh. Her straight face shows no trace even of a smile.

"Uh. Ms. ... I – well – you see – Pakistan is a country. I –."

"No. Pakistan is not a country, and we can only send wire transfers to recognized countries."

I'm dumbstruck. Did something happen today to Pakistan? Did it renounce its nationhood? Change its name? Was the entire country raptured? *Evangelicals were right after all.* Did it just vanish? Is this one of those dreams where next thing you know I look down and I'm still in my pajamas? What?

"Uh. You know, Ma'am. Pakistan, you know, is a country. It's right over there by those other *Stan* countries: Afghanistan. Tajikistan. Uzbekistan. Right above India on the map. Next to Iran. A little bit by China. Well, it doesn't border Tajikistan, really, there's this little strip — "

"I'm sorry, Mr. Demir. Pakistan is not a country. We can't send money to a place that does not have proper national channels, you understand."

"No, Ma'am. Honest. We actually have done so much good relief work in Pakistan. It is a country."

"No. It doesn't appear on our list of countries, the ones we recognize. We can only transfer to recognized countries."

"No. Ma'am. Really. Pakistan is part of the United Nations. It's actually a big country, lot of people."

At that moment — I swear this is the truth! — she has this television going, high up on the wall, and who comes on it? Here walks up President George W. Bush, on screen, in a press conference. And who strides up next to him? Pervez Musharraf, then-president of Pakistan. (Does he know his country has gone missing?)

It's a miracle! A sign! Problem solved!

"There! You see? That man on the left, next to President Bush. He's president of Pakistan. The country."

24

"I'm very sorry, Mr. Demir. I know what you're trying to say, but I don't make these lists. Just, Pakistan isn't a recognized country. So we can't send your wire. I'm sorry."

"No. Wait. You see that green flag, next to the American flag, has like a crescent moon on it? That's Pakistan's flag, the country flag. The two presidents are meeting, the two countries."

Bush is talking. He's saying the word "Pakistan" again and again.

"My hands are tied, Mr. Demir. It's not in my control. Let me put you in touch with the department that handles our wire transfers."

She makes the call.

"Oh? Oh. Oh, I see."

Hangs up.

"I'm sorry, Mr. Demir. (Laughs) Pakistan is a country. (Laughs again) That wire transfer's fine. It's the Palestine one that has the problem."

It'll be a long morning.

To Cry For

The general perception that *American institutions treat American Muslim charities just like other charities* is the biggest myth of them all, and no laughing matter. Banks especially put Muslim charities (and other Muslim-associated entities) through a relentless ringer of rolling U.S. Treasury Department regulations and roiling "de-risking" judgments. In bank-talk, "de-risking" means bank officers unilaterally close the accounts of any institution or individual they so much as sense exposes their institution to the threat of lawsuits and fines, possibly substantial, from the U.S. Government — and they do it without cause, explanation, or the account-holder's right of redress (even without any communication at all).

In practical reality, this means banks have the unilateral ability to shut down accounts of organizations and individuals based on mere suspicion and, therefore, to shut down the capacity of these organizations and individuals to function at the most basic level.

Though this process uses the mechanisms of law, it originates as politics, which is to say it is often driven or contaminated by partisan interests. Politicians in the executive and legislative branches and their powerful department and agency appointees create policies, sometimes unspoken or declared through guises — say, of national security or economic necessity — that end up punishing politically targeted vulnerable groups.

If your institution falls under such a looming political cloud, bank bureaucrats scurry to shed any risk of association with not only your organization but with you personally as a corporate officer and any account your individual name appears on, even the Girl Scouts Cookie Drive fund, and without any regard for the reality of your humanitarian agency's third-party-verified, stellar financial transactions history, its validated exemplary transparency, or even the life-threatening conditions of the needy who depend on its timely delivery of relief goods and payments. In a twinkling, financial institutions will toss your charity — its humanitarian recipients, its growth strategies, or even its existence — under a whole fleet of oncoming buses and into real and immediate existential peril, just to avoid the mere hint of a possibility that the government has your institution in its crosshairs, and no matter how unfairly a federal agency has targeted you.

Banks increasingly subject Muslim charities, businesses (and every last balance of the individuals associated with either) to account closings.

26

I am not speaking only of American banks, though as you read these words, U.S. financial institutions stand shamefully knee-deep in notices of "causeless" account closures sent to Muslim charities and other Muslim organizations and individuals for no other reason than these entities have some vague or superficial association with the name of the boogeyman of our time: *Muslim*. This emerging fiscal tsunami of *Muslim* de-risking runs right through the world banking system, as all international financial transactions depend on U.S. currency, which means that American regulators can pull almost any bank in the world into this rising (anti-) *Muslim* maelstrom in the tightly organized network that is the global monetary system.

This ends up exposing Muslims and their charities to the most removed guilt-by-association possible: Simply being *Muslim*. American Muslim charities now live a frightening fusion of Franz Kafka's *The Trial* and Joseph Heller's *Catch-22*: American Muslim humanitarian organizations help victims in global conflict zones. Most conflict zones in the world involve America, allied with some Muslims and fighting against others; and virtually all of these theaters of hostility create humanitarian crises that victimize tens, if not hundreds, of thousands of innocent Muslims.

"Counterterrorism frameworks" in America, Europe, and the world writ large "have engendered a sense of paralysis in parts of the humanitarian community," according to a March 2017 study by the Harvard Law School Program's Counterterrorism and Humanitarian Engagement Project.[*] The study goes on to state "some humanitarian actors report a 'chilling effect'" because of these laws and policies "on life-saving and needs-based humanitarian assistance."

Many relief agencies (and not just Muslim-run ones) will tell you, as the Harvard study indicates, that they perceive "counterterrorism laws and policies," which have wildly "proliferated over the past two decades," as "functioning in a way that could prohibit or otherwise impede forms of humanitarian action" that in principle they believe they should be undertaking. In hopeful news, there have been growing "perceptions across the expert philanthropic community that counterterrorism laws

---

[*]Pilot Empirical Survey Study on the Impact of Counterterrorism Measures on Humanitarian Action and Comment.

and policies are overly restrictive, vague, and far-reaching."

Nor does the Harvard survey appear as the first to report this fear in the humanitarian sector and the implications for the relief services its constituents offer. Nor does it provide the deepest analysis of this widespread sentiment. In 2013, independent researchers commissioned by the United Nations Office for the Coordination of Humanitarian Affairs (OCHA) and the Norwegian Refugee Council (NRC) showed extensive evidence of this increasing sense among aid agency workers in a *Study of the Impact of Donor Counterterrorism Measures on principled Humanitarian Action*. In a joint Foreword to this extensive study, then-OCHA Under-Secretary General Valerie Amos and NRC Secretary General Toril Brekke wrote:

> Certain donor counterterrorism measures have presented humanitarian actors with a serious dilemma. If we abide by our principles, we may break the law and face criminal prosecution. Adherence to some counterterrorism laws and measures may require us to act in a manner inconsistent with these principles. This could undermine the acceptance of humanitarian workers among the different parties engaged in conflict and the communities in which they work, preventing them from protecting and assisting those most in need. There is an urgent need to strike a better balance between the aims of counterterrorism laws and measures on one hand, and humanitarian action which adheres to these principles, on the other.

Double those stakes for American Muslim charities and their leaders. We live under a "terrorist" sword of Damocles — an accusation of abetting terrorism — hanging by the finest filament that federal agencies can cut at any moment by means of discrimination against Muslims, now broadly acceptable in America; or by dereliction of duty, in a frenzy of partisan opportunism or behind the blurred lines of an Evangelical nativism unexpectedly elevated to the apogee of American political power; or by means of pure delusion. American Muslim charities and their executives and aid workers have no margin of error to operate in, and no hope of gaining clarification or certainty through open discussion with bank and Treasury Department officers, no matter how we try or who we hire to try on our behalf.

I can tell you that we directors and staff of American Muslim charities rely totally on God for our security — and I know that is as it should be. Yet even the wisdom of religion encourages one to take things by their natural causes, which in this case, as the UN-Norwegian study points out, should constitute "sustained and open policy dialogue on how to better reconcile counterterrorism measures and humanitarian action."

I or any American Muslim charity principal (or Muslim humanitarian leaders anywhere in the world for that matter) could have written the top recommendation of the UN-Norwegian study. Yet we merely need to echo it: Frank discussion "should take place across all relevant sectors within government (security, justice, financial and humanitarian), as well as between States and the humanitarian community at both headquarters and field level."

Yet some five years on, a late-2017 study ordered by the European Commission (which we will look more closely at in the coming portions of this chapter) reports that American Muslim humanitarian stakeholders "have withdrawn providing services to populations in need out of fear of being implicated" by U.S. law enforcement officials and legislators "in the broad interpretation of material support" of our country's counterterrorism laws and policies. This European study's American scholars underscore how "significant" it is in this light "that a number of secular and Christian interlocutors" from American humanitarian agencies "did not report the same reservations or fears" about U.S. federal accusations that their Muslim counterparts did and "opted to continue their work." This includes the glaring discrepancy of "one non-Muslim organization's ability to distribute direct cash aid to beneficiaries in Iraq." Indeed, this group felt no threat of criminal liability at all or question of U.S. government suspicion, though providing "frontline aid distribution after the liberation of parts of Mosul in 2016." Yet when asked about doing the same, American Muslim charities — though the natural forebears of this humanitarian task, and perhaps more able and at least as eager to carry out such relief work — described this institutional war-zone presence "as beyond their political risk profile" in their own country, America.

Nothing flattens the morale of social fellowship and trust like watching charitable organizations that deliver less than 10 cents on the donated dollar to their recipients waltz through transfer protocols with barely a murmur, while your audited, four-star, financially compliant and certified transparent Muslim charity — which gives virtually 90 cents of every donated dollar to its beneficiaries — wallows in electronic no man's land, waiting for clueless clerks to press magic buttons that will send bread to a bloated child dying of starvation. *Every time? Every time?*

To have to prove your trustworthiness again and again, each episode anew — the authenticity of your local vendors; the validity of your delivery channels; the existence of the thousands of direly destitute your dutiful donors, sacrificing staff, and devoted volunteers serve — it absolutely poisons the heart. The UN-Norwegian study of 2013 rightfully "presented evidence that counterterrorism measures have had and continue to have a negative impact on humanitarian action." It documented a slew of humanitarian ethically "negative impacts" arising from ever-broadening and detailing counterterrorism laws and policies. These "range from halts and decreases in funding to blocking of projects, suspension of programs, planning and program design" that proceeded "not according to needs" but according to the political dictates of counterterrorism policy, which also caused "slowing of project implementation." This led, as well, to "beneficiaries in areas and structures" in various hotspots being "systematically excluded by some donors." In addition, "funding through Muslim charities … has been significantly obstructed."

That last telltale observation — Muslim charities being significantly obstructed — speaks directly to the discrimination American Muslim charities endure. The researchers' conclusion: "The implementation of counterterrorism laws as examined in this study undermines the neutrality, both real and perceived, of humanitarian actors, and the impartiality of their operations." This hypocritical subversion of American Muslim charities through the capricious, discriminatory implementation of America's counterterrorism laws and policies remains overwhelmingly true for American Muslim charities today, even more so than in 2013. It stems from an unacceptably and undeniably bigoted duplicity in the American federal and institutional system increasingly regulating the humanitarian sector.

Thank God for the antitoxin of patience for God's sake, the divine balm of faith in a Hereafter where God settles all accounts with justice and recompenses every good intent and injury suffered in the cause of sufficing a human being in want or pain. I refer you back to the words

30

of Jesus' 🕊 from the Beatitudes, which head this chapter. To them we may add: "Blessed are those who are persecuted for righteousness' sake, for theirs is the Kingdom of Heaven" (Matt. 5.10).

Still, this disparity in applying counterterrorism law and policy calls the question: *Why the difference?* Why does my top-performing charity meet with such profound, invented bureaucratic impediment when other immensely inefficient, questionably effective, enormously wasteful organizations see before them nothing but smiles and a parkway of green lights?

To Be a Muslim Humanitarian

In 2015, the European Commission initiated a three-year project to analyze countering violent extremism (CVE) in civil society called "Bridging Transatlantic Voices." Partnering with the British Council, Georgia State University (GSU), and the London-based Institute for Strategic Dialogue, the undertaking published one of its three major researches in November 2017: *The Muslim Humanitarian Sector*. The study could not be more crucial and makes a point that American governmental and humanitarian leaders simply must internalize, or continue doing soon-irreparable damage to the interests of this nation, not to mention tens of millions in our world caught up in unspeakable humanitarian catastrophe through no fault of their own:

> As can be seen through major international initiatives such as the Sustainable Development Goals, and the principles agreed upon at the 2016 World Humanitarian Summit, *a global consensus has emerged that faith based organizations (FBOs) are particularly poised to address a number of shared global challenges* rooted in problems of political conflict, violence, and extremism. …
>
> **Muslim aid NGOs in the United States have matured significantly**. … The sector has now positioned itself as **a key partner in the delivery of critical aid and relief to some of the most vulnerable populations around the world**.

Note my italics and boldface. Everyone sincerely at work in the humanitarian arena has recognized that we will not succeed in solving any of the source problems causing this unprecedented explosion on such a shocking scale of the victimization of innocent people in our conflicts without the inclusion of faith-based charities.

And what essential faith-based humanitarian aid cohort sits smack-dab in the middle of the world's major political-conflict/humanitarian-crisis nexus in the Middle East and North Africa (MENA) (as well as in Asia, in places like Kashmir and Myanmar (think Rohingya))? None other than your friendly neighborhood Muslim charities, of course — the very relief agencies our government-and-banking roulette wheelers and dealers relentlessly spin and stymie with their buckshot anti-terrorism money rules and blind blacklisting of crucial American Muslim charities by cowboy agents. In so doing, these blinkered and unbridled representatives gamble away their most reliable odds for advancing their stated interests, if we take their policy goals seriously.

> In order to overcome long-standing areas of misunderstanding and to better inform their decision-making for programming in the MENA region, policy makers and NGO practitioners should become better acquainted with the Muslim humanitarian landscape.

So reads the first recommendation of this study. Its authors have simply seen the on-the-ground reality that countless NGO workers snowboarding the building human avalanche of global suffering have known now for years. Our researchers' *Muslim Sector* study shows clearly that American Muslim charities in particular now represent the necessary pivot to "optimize the international community's response" to an "unprecedented set of humanitarian challenges it faces now and in the foreseeable future," and that this reality "demands attention and investment" be paid to and made in American Muslim charities "by all stakeholders."

American Muslim charities in general, and Zakat Foundation in particular, have forged serious and fruitful partnerships with so-termed "mainstream" humanitarian organizations, both faith-based and otherwise. Yet "when legal, logistical, and political problems emerge," for Zakat Foundation and other American Muslim charities, "it is often the case," this study finds, "that faith-based aid organizations from Muslim backgrounds bear the most burden of the problem."

Zakat Foundation partnerships have proven, almost since our inception, what this "research has found"; namely, "that aid and relief actors from both Christian and Muslim backgrounds share a common vision

32

of holistic community development." Like many among our Christian brothers and sisters in the relief struggle, Zakat Foundation humanitarian leaders and workers also see "our mandate as extending well beyond the period of delivering emergency services." Long after the media eye and the governmental gaze turn away from a crisis, the charitable hand of Zakat Foundation donors, and other American Muslim charities, remains steadfastly extended in "providing solutions for long-term economic growth and community sustainability" for the displaced, the destitute, and the devastated.

When our banking rep "lost" Pakistan as a nation in 2006, Afghan refugees in that country had hit one of the hardest periods of their long and hard-to-top suffering as migrants of war. At that time, "only 9 percent of Afghans in Pakistan reported having regular jobs, 55 percent of households depended on day labor for their livelihood, and 20 percent described themselves as self-employed," according to a June 2006 census by the United States Committee for Refugees and Immigrants. The report called Afghan refugee under-the-radar economic contribution so "significant" it kept the police from interfering in it.

Yet it paints a picture of local Pakistani community abuse of vulnerable refugees, especially women NGO workers, female-headed households, and child street workers. It describes a climate among Pakistanis not unfamiliar to us now in America, where refugees bear undocumented but widely believed blame for high crime rates, lack of employment, and negative cultural change.

Pakistan officials, in fact, turned a blind eye to this exploitation and perpetrated a climate of ill-treatment and unwelcome for migrants to foment support for its new policy of repatriation of its building Afghan refugee population, which climbed by a million people to 2,035,023 in 2007, the highest number of Afghan refugees ever registered in Pakistan.

In May of 2006, Musharraf requested that the United Nations repatriate all Afghan refugees. With that cover, his government then instituted the coercive conditions to make this a reality. Refugees received eviction notices en masse, while a policy of systematic police harassment put the unwritten exclamation point to the expulsions. They razed refugee homes to the ground, beat families, including children, and entirely shut down 32 camps housing more than 400,000 refugees along the Afghan border and around Islamabad in the name of national security. Only refugees wealthy enough to pay massive bribes to authorities remained in the areas marked for cleansing.

The Pakistani government then claimed that 450,000 Afghan refugees — legitimately frightened of even deeper poverty and retribution in their home country — "volunteered" to return to their war-zone homes.

At this time, NGOs like Zakat Foundation stood as the only path to education for Afghan children in a country that signed on to the Convention on the Rights of Children but prevented Afghan children from attending public schools. Some 170,000 Afghan camp children had their human right to education immediately jeopardized. Pakistan shut down some schools and banished "all foreigners" from them.

Refugee healthcare services similarly suffered. Humanitarian relief organizations provided first-rate healthcare — better than offered in the country at large or in Afghanistan — to the dwellers of more than 100 camps, according to the UN refugee agency UNHCR. Healthcare agencies also employed more than 5,000 refugee workers.

If you seek a point to my recounting of these tragic numbers of a dozen years past, take this into consideration first: American youth who begin their military service in 2019 will have come into the world a year *after* the U.S. War in Afghanistan began on October 7, 2001 — now in its 18th year as of this writing. The longest American war in history, pundits have dubbed it *The Forever War*, after Vietnam veteran Joe Haldeman's 1974 allegorical Science Fiction classic, and also "The Forgotten War" because Pentagon officials have asked not to receive questions on it anymore and obliging American reporters rarely cover it.

In March 2019, the conflict took its place as the longest participation of U.S. combat forces anywhere ever, surpassing Vietnam (and with no end in sight, as President Trump has increased troop levels to 14,000 and, at the NATO Summit in Brussels on July 12, 2018, reportedly gave assurances to keep them there, along with NATO leaders committing to fund the conflict through 2024).

Historians have not nicknamed Afghanistan the graveyard of empires for nothing. As of July 2018, America has spent an incomprehensible $1.07 trillion on it, 2,372 soldiers have died, another 1,720 U.S. civilian contractors have perished, and the war has left a staggering 20,320 American service members wounded in action. One shudders at the estimate ranges by some of the total number of Afghans killed: 640,000 to 1.4 million (MintPress News, April 3, 2018).

By now, everyone from the President down to the last taxpayer knows this war is unwinnable. Violence does not, in the end, bring about victory. How many magnitudes of military might does *uberdeveloped*, technologically magical America have over destitute, demolished, primitive Afghanistan? Hope in the unseen — a future awaiting a people beleaguered by nearly half a century of winless conflict — that is the deliverer of triumph. The men and women of Afghanistan need to see tomorrow's clear horizon of possibility, for themselves and their children. People without such a vision turn violent in their hunger, their poverty, their victimization by war.

With this in mind, our Zakat Foundation donors sponsored 400 university students, boys and girls, to build Afghanistan's future as teachers, social scientists, nurses, doctors, religious scholars, linguists, engineers, historians, biologists, physical scientists — the human cornerstones of learning that can serve as new building blocks for a ruined society. We worked with partner organizations that could see to these students' accommodations and necessities. Afghanistan offers free education, but its rural area poor lack the means to send and sustain their children in the major cities that have universities. Our donors' contributions rented the dorms for them, provided their food, covered the cost of their books and supplies, paid for their living incidentals — for years. I cannot stress enough the importance of this ongoing charitable program for Afghanistan.

One day in 2015, our bank informed us it would no longer send money to Afghanistan. No problem on our end or among our recipient student scholars triggered this. The money transfer simply ceased. It did not hurt Zakat Foundation. It did not affect our donors, American Muslims and others. It did not reduce our support. It simply devastated the lives of the lifelong beleaguered Afghan young men and women on the receiving end of an American humanitarian agency's aid.

This began the banking persecution of Zakat Foundation and other American Muslim charities. Soon our banks, and then others we sought help from, refused to wire our payments to many countries, or sought to prevent our charitable monetary transactions for relief of the suffering in various financial forms. Here, the sick could not buy their medicine.

There, the refugee could no longer resettle for the future. This widow had nothing to purchase food for her children. That father displaced by famine could only sit and watch his children waste away.

Like Zakat Foundation, other American Muslim charities soon found themselves facing an unspoken wire transfer ban. The Better Business Bureau may have graded you a top organization. Charity Navigator might have given you its prime four-star charity rating, as it did Zakat Foundation. Your bank officers themselves may have approved your institution's financial transparency, praised your charity's openness. Other American charities, religious and secular, may have awarded you their top humanitarian awards for "carrying on Abraham Lincoln's legacy by fighting modern-day slavery," or for "building bridges between faith groups," or for "performing an extraordinary act of saving a life," or for "helping large numbers of people in the world," as did SWIFT in according me its "Faith in Humanity Award." InterAction may recognize your institution as part of its vaunted "Together Project." Your organization may be a key supporter of the Charity and Security Network's financial access research. International diplomats may have applauded your charity. Government ministers across the world may have hailed it. Celebrity philanthropists like Martin Sheen and U2 lead singer Bono may have expressed their spiritual honor to join in "asking God to bless everyone connected to the Foundation" for its powerful impact on the lives of refugees. The U.S. State Department may have lauded it. Former president George H.W. Bush himself may have thanked you for your institution's "amazing work" for its distinguished, firsthand help of inundated Houstonians after Hurricane Harvey — all of which applies to Zakat Foundation, yet none of which is relevant to this complex of counterterrorism laws, suspicion of Muslims, and our fearful financial system.

Somewhere in your heart, you may think, well, terrorism in the Middle East and North Africa, you know, it's a tough issue. Let me wipe this from your mind. As I write this, Chicago has just experienced one of the bloodiest weekends of violence in its history. An astounding 33 separate shootings killed 12 and wounded 62, the youngest victim an 11-year-old girl, the eldest, a man, 62. The gun mayhem happened mainly in four West and South Side communities — right where Zakat Foundation sought to buy a bank-possessed, longtime school building in

2017 to open a vocational school, subsidized by our donors, to build the massive talents yet bleak futures of the impoverished youth there, to make a difference in our Chicagoland home community because we American Muslims care. We serve the poor, the needy, the downtrodden, the disaster-stricken — not only overseas but here at home, in America, for these families, these people, these communities who we call neighbors, colleagues, and friends. I cannot express to you the level of love and rising concern American Muslims have for their fellow citizens and our society here.

Yet that is exactly when Bank of America (the "Life's better when we're connected" people) — an institution we'd been "connected" with as Zakat Foundation for five years — suddenly could not get our wire transfer of payment for the school building through to the title company. Not across the sea. Not into a war zone in the Middle East. Not into a district controlled by a U.S.-designated terrorist group, but basically across town, for God's sake, in the middle of Chicago, into a district where the title company's BMO bank (the "We're here to help for all life's moments, no matter how big or small" people) kept its account, the same BMO with whom Zakat Foundation also had an account for this big-time, game-changing event in "life's moments" for Chicago's South Side disenfranchised, to lay down for them a runway to soar above the guns and the despair and the colossal cry for dignity, to be lives that matter, that underlie all the shootings and death.

Do not blame Zakat Foundation for this tragic system failure. Such is the financial matrix and counterterrorism madness — its Muslim mania — run amok. We professionally assessed the South Side situation. We talked to the local people's political representatives. We consulted their community leadership. We brought the church groups and the mosque bodies together and into the project. We identified up and down and all around what we needed to do for these community kids and young men and women who face skyrocketing youth unemployment, soaring crime rates, a gushing prison pipeline — social earthquakes shaking the unstable ground beneath their feet. Every community stakeholder and concerned observer concluded together that Zakat Foundation donors should build this community a vocational school. Give local students a trade: a skill for their hands, a means for their minds, a living, a path to jobs or to open businesses, wings out of poverty, a channel to serve their neighbors, and to feed and house and stabilize their families. Do it for the sake of God.

So we did it, for God's sake. We had all the funding in place, every last dime of it coming from our donors, American citizens. Every single cent of this organization registered. No monies coming to this project from outside entities. We keep no foreign accounts. We made the down payment. We did our 30-day due diligence, professional inspections by city-approved specialists — infrastructure, vital utilities, contamination assessments — all clear. We gave our proposal to the appointed court receiver assigned to manage the affairs of this bank-owned property. We went through every step of the court-regulated processes. Others had offered to purchase the property, but the bank and receiver deemed our plan most attractive, and it was. The community supported us. Its political leadership supported us. The neighborhood organizers supported us. The local institutions supported us. The authorities sent our approved offer to the bank owner. They formally accepted. We signed the contract. We gave the title company due information. We sent the money to their account. Done!

Except … Big Brother.

After three days, the title company informed us they had received no funds. We called Bank of America. "Where's the money?"

"We sent it." Bank officers showed us it left the account.

We waited — five days, a week, 10 days. The money never arrived in the title company's account. We talked with Bank of America. We inquired with BMO. Officers of the former then told us they believed the federal government had inserted itself. They advised patience. Let it clear.

It never happened. The money bounced back to our Bank of America account. No explanation. No word as to who deflected it. No account of what legal mechanism, if any, had been applied. No identification as to who blocked it and under what authority.

Our 80-year-old, local attorney told us that in 50 years of real estate practice he had never seen anything like it, where no cause, elucidation, justification, or answers accompanied so bizarre a "non-rejection," as if it never happened. Nothing. Not a syllable. Just a black hole. A financial dark op.

I tried to write the title company a check. They refused, fearing the federal government. We couldn't even put cash in an escrow account for them. We lost the property. Chicago's South Side community watched another promise vanish into thin air. Their trapped sons and daughters saw it all go up in what they know best — gun smoke, the ringing of semi-automatic fire, unmistakable proof that no one out there cares for them. My heart broke. Cry, these beloved children.

Then it all came down. Bank of America had stopped sending our regular wire transfers overseas, a small amount of money to fund Zakat Foundation humanitarian projects. We shifted to BMO. The same payment had continued automatically for years by this time. A BMO representative one day calls me.

"Why are you sending this money there?"

"That's what we've always done. It's been regular for years."

"I'm very sorry," he says. "I don't know why I have to ask you this stupid question. I know that's what you have always done. You send the money, and you use it for overseas projects. I apologize."

I understood from this conversation that he had received an inquiry from a dark room somewhere, asking about our transfer, a simple question for the banker to answer. "It's what they've always done." Same pattern. Nothing extraordinary. But the banker didn't think? Didn't check? Or feared answering.

Within days, Bank of America sent us a letter. They would "de-risk" from Zakat Foundation. They gave us 30 days to retrieve the funds. That was August 2017. In September, I received another letter from BMO. They, too, had decided to "de-risk." Then, these banks closed every single account affiliated in any way with my name. When I mentioned the Girl Scout account previously, I wasn't being facetious or hyperbolic. A friend of mine had a Girl Scout-related account I had to remove my name from, or the bank would close it.

But then a funny thing happened. Truth finds a way. When BMO sent us its account closure letter, it inadvertently included in our Zakat Foundation envelope the letters of other "Muslim-named" accounts it simultaneously had closed. The machine made a mistake. The bank pogrom was on. The federal government had taken the decision to cripple or close, by surreptitious means of de-banking and financial obstruction, Muslim humanitarian and other organizations.

So much for liberty, free capital and entrepreneurship, and public-spirited philanthropy. Not so different, the youth of Afghanistan and the young of America, if you look like the boys and girls of Chicago's West and South sides. Perhaps George Orwell's *Animal Farm* has meaning, not just for Stalinist-era Russia, but in America today, after all. *All animals are equal. But some animals are more equal than others.*

But what do I know, someone who grew up a poor Kurdish kid? I guess democracy applies differently to different people.

Muslim Charities — A New Arch Stone of the Humanitarian Sector

Many in government, finance, and humanitarian service now express genuine alarm by the wildfire spread of conflict and crisis in the world and its horrific human fallout. Look at these United Nations numbers: 68.5 million people displaced; 127 million starving or headed toward its brink and another 815 million chronically undernourished; 2.1 billion without safe drinking water; 4.5 billion lacking safe sanitation; 5.6 million children 5 and younger dying annually from disease and malnutrition, almost half in Africa and a quarter in Southeast Asia; and an estimated 24.9 million human trafficking victims, according to the International Labor Organization and Walk Free Foundation 2017 report.

Marie Juul Peterson studied Muslim NGOs and noted a trajectory of rapid development of Muslim humanitarian organizations as a result of their key stages of development through the 1980s Somalia famine, the Afghan-Soviet conflict, the war in Bosnia, and their trial by fire in the aftermath of September 11. To this list, the Georgia State University *Muslim Sector* authors add Muslim charitable institutions' need to confront the rise of ISIS, the Syrian civil war, and Myanmar's shocking Rohingya ethnic cleansing in their work.

The results of Muslim charities running this 40-year gauntlet of growth, according to that study, now stand clear: "The Muslim aid sector is now poised to deliver radically innovative solutions to global poverty, the forced migration crisis, and sustainable development."

God knows it's needed. The time has come, they add, for "stakeholders to recognize that Muslim aid organizations" bring urgently needed additional benefits to the global crisis table, "especially those headquartered in North America and Europe." Those of us privileged to serve in these Muslim charities have made considerable headway turning them into "critical sites of cultural encounter and civic engagement" for

40

groups long separated by misunderstandings and an inertia of opposition. Our *Muslim Sector* authors astutely observe that this experience "can be further explored" to see what works in "civil society approaches" that reinforce "social cohesion," thereby "transforming conflict" into communal cooperation.

The promise of transformation and togetherness that Muslim humanitarian institutions hold for the world, however, cannot come to fruition without expanding the space of our "financial access for humanitarian" activity and giving us elbow room to function "in fragile contexts" that simply do not present the clear lines that an unreasonable and self-defeating "outgrowth of post-9/11 counterterrorist finance (CTF) policies" assume. And what have these policies of state control brought us but an incessantly encroaching micromanagement by financial institutions of their nonprofit sector clients, to the point that they have monetarily hamstrung us and crippled our desperately needed relief work. I contend a causal relationship between *these policies* and *increased conflict* and the eruption of *humanitarian crises*. Nor am I alone in seeing this:

> Experts note that while these measures have significantly increased the capacity of international law enforcement agencies to restrict the freedom of terrorist networks, it has also adversely impacted the freedom of civil society actors to positively influence the social and political recovery of the conflict-stricken MENA region. *An emerging consensus is forming among regulatory bodies, civil society advocates as well as security analysts that significant reforms to counterterrorism finance policies are urgently needed to meet their shared human and national security goals.* (*Muslim Sector*, p. 17, italics added)

All through this book, and even in the present chapter, I've specifically addressed the discriminatory myths assailing the American Muslim charity. But what I speak to now does not only harm us, it injures relief agencies across the board and global humanitarian work everywhere. Like all things of this nature, it began with the vulnerable then grew to engulf the whole.

That's what a 2017 Charity and Securities Network (CSN) "Financial Access" report quantifies: Two in three U.S. nonprofits doing relief work internationally report consequential ongoing issues with banks that disrupt their programs, including wire-transfer delays, peculiar requests for documents, and account closures. The CSN assessment also finds that especially those nonprofits at work "in peace operations/peace-building, public health, development/poverty reduction, human rights/democracy-building, and humanitarian relief report the greatest difficulties."

So counterterrorism policy discrimination not only extends to who you identify as or with (though you can believe the spotlight never dims on Muslim charities), its focus lies more on whom you serve and where they live — because it follows the arc of the political ax as it falls and the places on which it comes down hardest.

The Harvard Law School Program's Counterterrorism and Humanitarian Engagement Project March 2017 study mentioned previously confirms these CSN findings. Researchers surveyed some 500 individuals at varying levels of humanitarian organizations in nearly 50 countries and territories in the world. Fully 60 percent confirmed that "counterterrorism laws affected their respective organization's commitment and adherence to the humanitarian principles of humanity, impartiality, independence, and neutrality." A whopping "91 percent of respondents answered that it weakened their commitment to humanitarian principles, suggesting a strong perceived impact of counterterrorism laws and policies on the work of humanitarians." And if you feel that cold counterterrorism law breeze freezing your bones, know that 69 percent of survey respondents felt it too; they "indicated that counterterrorism measures had chilled or curtailed their [humanitarian] work," while 38 percent of respondents affirmed that their humanitarian organizations just gave up, or at least gave in; they "stated that counterterrorism laws had caused their organization to forgo, alter, or cease activities and programming."

Commenting on this, *Muslim Sector* study authors noted that "when legitimate actors abandon their humanitarian operations in critical environments because their traditional means of financial access are restricted, the most vulnerable and marginalized communities suffer the most." Even more to the point, the enforcers of counterterrorism laws and policies actually abet the very people they claim to want to foil. (Should *they* have their accounts closed?) Their enforcement causes "increased security risks [that] emerge when legitimate actors, forced out of utilizing conventional financial services," leave behind "a vacuum … in fragile and deteriorating environments … often filled by illegal actors whose social and political practices increase the propensity for violence, conflict, and human suffering." Moreover, by hampering their own Muslim charities and other humanitarian organizations, "new regional and global geopolitical actors" step into the spaces typically "under the purview of North American and European political influence."

The question is this: *Where do our global counterterrorism finance and anti-money laundering laws leave us*, as applied by our governments, legislators, and federal agencies to Muslim charities and other humanitarian organizations? Here's the three-part prediction of the entire brain trust of academics, practitioners, and humanitarian legal advocates that the *Muslim Sector* researches consulted.

They will:

1. Continue to reduce the provision of beneficiary services to populations in need.
2. Exacerbate conflict and fragility by ceding control of aid zones to non-vetted actors.
3. Lead to a net loss of geopolitical influence for European and North American countries.

This leads to a single, obvious conclusion:

It is imperative that policy makers at the highest level of government and intergovernmental organizations place the integrated issues of financial access, development, and security on the top of their list of priorities in order to meet their human and national security goals in the short, medium, and long-term. (*Muslim Sector*, p. 19)

In other words, facilitate for and work with your Muslim charities and your humanitarian organizations, even as they have begun to integrate and work with one another, instead of terrorizing them with your counterterrorism laws and incapacitating them. They offer a hand of help to both war's afflicted *and* the best interests of this nation.

Who Gives a FATF?

The Financial Action Task Force (FATF): Ooh! Just saying the name scares you. For humanitarian relief charities, FATF looms as the most powerful and pernicious entity in the world. Atop all the other regulatory bodies, domestic and international, FATF bears most responsibility for impairing the humanitarian function of global relief agencies in settings susceptible to conflict with their delicate communal balances.

Founded in 1990 by the G-7 and housed within the Organization for Economic Cooperation and Development (OECD), its intergovernmental agency members make policy recommendations to fortify the international financial system, especially against money laundering and terrorist finance. Though FATF proposals hold no binding authority over any country, it nonetheless has grown to dominate financial policy over more than 200 global states and authorities (including the Holy See) with its 40(+9) detailed "recommendations." Its might morphed immensely after September 11, 2001, when it began advocating U.S. Patriot Act measures globally. For all its influence, FATF itself remains unregulated and opaque to all outside evaluation.

By 2011, a raft of new and exceptionally restrictive NGO rules of operation emerged in autocratic countries and conflict zones around the world that few knew the origin of. Aid organizations did discover the work of their local partner institutions in these crucial areas suddenly and critically impeded by ghost regulations that seemed, after examination, directly aimed at curtailing the civil work of and gaining control over humanitarian nonprofits and their grantors.

FATF, of course, turned up behind these directives. Its infamous Special Recommendation VIII (SR VIII) puts nonprofits and, therefore, civil society itself squarely under the thumb of autocratic governments and nominally democratic administrations envious of their imperious power. They can license nonprofits, approve their funding from sources outside the country, and withdraw their permits at any time. It reads, in part:

> Countries should review the adequacy of laws and regulations that relate to entities that can be abused for the financing of terrorism. Nonprofit organizations are particularly vulnerable, and countries should ensure that they cannot be misused: (i) by terrorist organizations posing as legitimate entities; (ii) to exploit legitimate entities as conduits for terrorist financing, including for the purpose of escaping asset freezing measures; and (iii) to conceal or obscure the clandestine diversion of funds intended for legitimate purposes to terrorist organizations.

In the wake of the application of this rule, India, for example, modified its authority under R8 (and to the documented extolling of the U.S. Treasury officials hoping it "would provide an excellent example to other countries in South Asia") to rightfully withdraw NGO permits that the government unilaterally designated as "organizations of a political nature." Just two years later, the Indian government did exactly that, wiping out north of 4,000 NGOs with a mere pronouncement. Those 800 Tamil Nadu nonprofits protesting a nuclear site … they disappeared that day (see Open Society Foundations, *Voices*, May 8, 2013. "From Countering Financial Crime to Criminalizing Civil Society: How the FATF Overstepped the Mark").

Zakat Foundation joined a group of NGOs, humanitarian foundations, and donors that lobbied the World Bank, and others in their respective countries, to endorse a statement of concern that R8 "is being used as justification to suppress the activities of legitimate [nonprofits] and charitable and civil society organizations." FATF succumbed (somewhat) and revised R8 in 2016 to climb down from unilateral enforcement to "proportionate" measures in line with "risk-based" assessment, which, of course, does nothing for Muslim charities, as we constitute the poster-children for the myth of terrorist risk. You may alternatively read FATF's modification as *just make sure you keep your Muslim charities financially disabled.*

Yet even for relief agencies other than Muslims, FATF's damage is done, loosed upon the financial sector down to the local level, with banks who have their collective foot on the jugular of humanitarian monetary system access. The U.S. government, *Muslim Sector* study scholars say, would have to impose sweeping changes if it wants to redirect commercial banks away from this embedded behavior hobbling international humanitarian institutions. They recommend "ministerial level and direct intergovernmental intervention … to accelerate and encourage the re-opening of civil society spaces … curtailed by the broad reach of SR VIII."

A persuasive assessment by the Transnational Institute's Ben Hayes — damningly titled "Counter-Terrorism, 'Policy Laundering' and FATF: Legalizing Surveillance, Regulating Civil Society" — puts it less delicately. Forgive me for quoting from it at some length, but, in fact, anyone concerned with the brave new humanitarian world according to FATF ought to read this report in its entirety. It is that important:

> The "top-down" and over-broad approach to the regulation of civil society in the name of countering terrorism, strongly promoted by U.S. governments and the Financial Action Task Force, clearly contradicts these values and principles [of fundamental freedom

for civil society and individuals all over the world]. … The research demonstrates that, in its current form, FATF SR VIII is a danger to civil society organizations in many parts of the world, because it incites governments to introduce onerous rules and regulations, subject NPOs [nonprofit organizations] to excessive state surveillance, and interfere in or restrict the activities of CSOs [civil society organizations]. … That is what the FATF process has resulted in. An innocuous sounding Recommendation "on reducing the vulnerability of the NPO sector to the vulnerability of terrorist financing" from an obscure intergovernmental body has been interpreted, expanded and enforced in a way that threatens to impose a rigid global framework for state regulation of NPOs.

A growing body of research has documented the way in which many less developed and less democratic states already make it very difficult for NPOs to operate without undue restraint; many of their governments now have the express endorsement of the FATF, World Bank or IMF to introduce or expand regulatory frameworks that facilitate their intrusions into activities of NGOs and civil society organizations. The plethora of rules and regulations regarding due diligence and the proactive disclosure of suspicions about terrorist links has also made it much more difficult for international NGOs and donor organizations to work in conflict zones and with "suspect communities". … *This can only have negative consequences for social justice and conflict resolution initiatives that had previously benefited from projects supporting grass-roots and community organizations and engaging marginalized stakeholders.* …

In imposing a package that amounts to wholesale NPO regulation in order to serve an international law enforcement agenda, the FATF has also disregarded the great strides toward transparency and accountability already taken by NPO sectors in many countries. State-centric approaches also ignore the positive role that NPOs can play in both assessing measures to prevent terrorist financing and ensuring that any new regulations [do] not impact adversely on others in civil society. The FATF's approach to the NPO sector contrasts [with] that taken toward the banking and financial services sectors, which have long had observer status at the FATF and play a very active role in the development and implementation of FATF Recommendations. It is difficult to understand why the recommendation, guidance and evaluation criteria for SR VIII have all been drawn-up by the FATF without any open consultation or structured input from concerned NPOs.

FATF raises questions even beyond this severe indictment. How, for example, does it endorse as *praiseworthy and effective* military junta-run countries and kingdoms — which have virtually no civil society that does not exist at the discretion of state — while its nearly blanket anti-nonprofit stance of suspicion and de-risking faults and harms totally transparent, upright charities like Zakat Foundation?

In fact, FATF's recommendations, and counterterrorism financing in general, constitute a complex ineffective sham. They accomplish oppressive state control while delivering nothing in the way of the security they purport to bolster.

Says Peter Neumann, director of the International Centre for the Study of Radicalization and Political Violence at Kings College, London: "There is no evidence that [CTF] has ever thwarted a terrorist campaign."

Thoughts of an American Muslim Humanitarian

The misconception that *American Institutions Treat Muslim Charities Just Like Other Charities* finds its basis in an even more prevalent and fundamentally dangerous perception: A 1996 CIA document whose title — "Report on NGOs with Terror Links" — itself asserts a now ubiquitous falsehood that it may be too late for our generation to alter in the public mind. This fiction "helped establish the now pervasive myth that Muslim aid and development organizations and charities are disproportionately used as fronts for terrorist activity," according to the *Muslim Sector* inquiry, citing the study *Islam and Development: Exploring the Invisible Aid Economy*, edited by Australian scholars Matthew Clarke and David Tittensor, which, with the writings of its 9 researchers and the themes and case studies they explore, wisely seeks to re-contextualize the charitable giving of Muslims in their religion.

How ironic that "an al-Qaeda-centric model" that has exerted such extensive influence on "policy thinking, intelligence gathering, and law enforcement activities" when it comes to "Muslim humanitarian organizations in and around conflict zones," now dictates attitudes and practices toward Muslim charities within the United States, as evidenced by Zakat Foundation's government-aborted attempted Chicago vocational school purchase and local community investment in an area that sorely needs it. This two-decade-old CIA-write-up's simple-minded, unvetted, erroneous presumption of a "regular correlation between Muslim humanitarian organizations and terrorist activity" — which shows nothing more than chauvinism — still underpins a global policy of transgressing the civil rights of American Muslim charities and their donors and seriously undermines the work of and contributors to other humanitarian organizations, even as it tramples the human rights to relief and aid of countless millions across the planet.

Or is it ironic?

This much is sure. Faceless, impenetrable, unaccountable inter-government agencies virtually absent from the public consciousness now wage a massive and sustained assault against civil society in the world, not least of all here in America. Social division at all our human fault lines appears as the natural byproduct, if not the strategy, of this will to suppress the native human impulse to organize to better the human condition and ease the apprehensions of people. Yet the "effect of this al-Qaeda-centric logic," the *Muslim Sector* report correctly observes, has created just the opposite dynamic between concerned citizens and among charitable groups; that of "exacerbated tensions" followed by a diminished "capacity for trust building among" Muslim charities, other faith-based and secular nonprofits, and the institutional and state "actors in the global humanitarian sector."

Divide and conquer?

The intelligence the Quran gives us about such repressive mentalities reveals the social mechanism to despotism of the archetypal tyrant himself, Pharaoh of ancient Egypt. ❨Indeed, Pharaoh exalted himself in the land and segregated its people into factions, oppressing a group of them. … Indeed, he was of those who sowed corruption on earth❩ (Sûrat Al-Qaṣaṣ, 28:4).

Muslim humanitarians are weary of the societal factionalizing that depends upon the now obvious and oft-proven falseness inherent in the "persistence of [the] accusations that [our] organizations [are] linked to, or affiliated with, terrorist activity," which the *Muslim Sector* study cites Muslim humanitarian leaders collectively saying. We have sophisticated over the preceding two decades and worked diligently in that time to show beyond any and all doubt that this imputation falls flat against the demonstrable facts of our scrupulously documented finances, the open record of our work, the firsthand witness of our partners in the field, and our meticulously studied religion and religious convictions, which stand unequivocally against terrorism as either a means or as an end. This most slanderous of "assumptions that the Muslim humanitarian sector is prone to terrorist manipulation" has even "resulted in high-profile cases of failed investigations and prosecutions." Personally devastating and organizationally damaging though they are, these cases (especially when closely critiqued against actual fact and law) nonetheless repeatedly vindicate Muslim charities collectively all the more. Still, their occurrences serve only to "further erode the capacity for cooperation." In the face of all this evidence and attestation to the contrary, the terrorist Muslim charity "stereotypes have gotten worse over time and have led to [increased] discriminatory behavior." Who can blame the Muslim donor if he or she hesitates to give to our charities when the "material support statutes and the threat of terrorist designation have loomed [so] large over domestic and transnational civil society organizations and especially those working in fragile and conflict contexts"?

But let us look to the positive groundswell now forming beneath the surface turbulence of political power's will to subdue the *humane* nature of ordinary people with and for one another. Many prominent voices now rise in sharp censure of the sweeping and coercive applications of the tools of state control and agency jurisdiction over the common good. "Former U.S. President Jimmy Carter, Human Rights Watch, and the International Crisis Group" have all warned against "such a broad interpretation of the law" of material support as undermining the very meaning of American democracy. It "not only violates free speech but also works" at cross purposes against the stated aims of these regulations to begin with, exacerbating instead of "reducing conflict."

Moreover, as the *Muslim Sector* study points out, the aggressive implementation of material support laws works best, not at drying up supposed sources of clandestine funding, but at "dissolving the critical and obvious distinction between criminal agents," few and far between, who would aid terrorist organizations as opposed to the plethora of "individuals or groups aiming to mediate conflict and build peace in fragile environments."

We who lead these Muslim charities well know that "no amount of documentation, reporting, and transparency" will ever 'be enough' to satisfy the insatiable bureaucratic appetites of regulators and banks working *over* instead of *with* us. We recognize that lawmakers and bureaucrats had us in mind when they "specifically targeted and overburdened" us in the "post-9/11 regulatory environment." We understand, as a 2014 Harvard study of humanitarian institutions points out, that these overseers have no concern that they have heartlessly diverted us into "devoting more resources to the administrative, policy, operational, and legal components" to prove we do not secretly divert our funds to terrorists, instead of allowing us to "revert" those humanitarian gifts to their rightful owners: the desperately poor, starving, sick, displaced, widowed, and orphaned, the needy whom these donations actually targeted and to whom they factually belong. Yet these functionaries, properly designated as *public servants*, seek instead to drive us along the endless paper trail of tears to the point of "compliance fatigue." To all this would they compel us, as the 2014 Harvard study notes, while their regimen "in many respects" stands complicit in reducing us to "fewer resources" and bringing us "under increasingly greater scrutiny from donors and the media."

Muslim charities have a habit of landing on their feet, and can now boast an often better record than their counterpart humanitarian institutions in "meeting and even surpassing the compliance standards of the NGO sectors in the United States and the U.K." Even so, "Muslim aid and development sectors continue to be falsely accused of harboring ties to extremist organizations."

The *Muslim Sector* study cites a flabbergasting example of American lawmakers' readiness to accuse Muslim charities of abetting extremism that rises to the level of clinical psychosis. When Hurricane Irma struck Florida in September 2017 and the bill to fund its disaster relief went to U.S. Congress, "Florida representative Rob DeSantis introduced an amendment into the bill specifically identifying that no such monies should go to Islamic Relief." Never mind that many deemed his rider "unconstitutional" (and that Islamic Relief does truly wonderful domestic humanitarian work). It took a "concerted effort by dozens of charities and advocacy groups" to white out his language, "a stark reminder of the continued political challenges the sector faces."

᠈ᡨᠵᡪ

As an American Muslim humanitarian, I cannot help but think of a group from the previous century I find our experience most analogous to: the Jews of Europe. The parallels between American Muslims in the first decades of this century and the European Jews of a similar timeframe in the 20th produce an uncanny resonance. This would be unnerving were it not for the lifelong insight the Quran has provided me through the eyes of the prophets and their followers as it recounts their real and invariably harrowing histories.

In this regard, Hannah Arendt has something to tell us in her reflections from 1950 on *The Origins of Totalitarianism*:

> Comprehension [of history and happenings] does not mean denying the outrageous, deducing the unprecedented from precedents, or explaining phenomena by such analogies and generalities that the impact of reality and the shock of experience are no longer felt. It means, rather, examining and bearing consciously the burden that our century has placed on us — neither denying its existence nor submitting meekly to its weight. Comprehension, in short, means the unpremeditated, attentive facing up to, and resisting of, reality — whatever it may be.

In our century, I think this means confronting an uncomfortable truth, especially for Americans: An elite is scapegoating Muslims to consolidate power over people. Yoking Muslims to terrorism in the public mind gives them a rationale to usurp the common and necessary rights of civil society. Gradually, it is becoming illegal for ordinary citizens to organize for any purposes that address their natural concerns for other human beings, especially across borders, and to act in concert with their beliefs to relieve the harsh conditions of others without permission from some authority. In this way, those entrusted with power steadily harvest the free human energies of the populace to serve in their fields of personal or partisan aims and interests in the now hallowed names of national security and domestic economy.

Those of us working in the humanitarian vineyards of American Muslim charities already endure this tribulation of persecution. Yet in the

51

plain of our spirits, the Quran plants vistas that unfurl before us to cool our eyes, that our sacrifices, though beleaguering and sometimes frightening, shall not seed into the earth in vain but grow up with our reward. ❨Indeed, those who have come to you with the wicked slander are a band of hypocrites among you. Do not consider it evil for you. But, rather, it is good for you❩ (Sûrat Al-Nûr, 24:11).

In the worldly fields of our humanitarian service, however, I believe it important — rather, vital — that we continue our strive to bring the fruit God has bestowed for safekeeping with some of us to those others whom He has actually created it for, so that we can know the humility of handing it over with head bowed to Him to its deserving; and know then, too, the joy of the sense it opens between us and another, as if having found our long-lost human brotherhood.

I confess gratitude for the blessed striving I have known in this human work of the Divine, which has brought me hand-in-hand, and racing knee-to-knee, with others working this selfsame blessing, driven separately in their faiths, their convictions, by their moral imperatives to reach first (or also) that needful soul awaiting equally his right on us as a man, or her provision sent down from the skies into our hands, or to deliver this child's milk and that one's honey.

A solidarity — no, let me have the heart to call it what it is — *a human love* has grown among the servants in the humanitarian community. In it, I see righteousness (and you have borne witness to its voices calling out from these pages). From it, I hear truth (and it speaks ever louder with a clear, crystalline honesty in the face of public wrath and personal risk). I behold valor (and feel humility before the courage of those who stand, one after the other, to defend these Muslim charities, these Muslim givers, these Muslim recipients, me, while they themselves may not be Muslim). I see human fellowship (and it looks out to me from eyes of every color, calls out to me with tongues of countless dialects, and reaches out to me with hands of every feel and hue).

This brings us back to the perennial truths with which we began (and *for which* we began our humanitarian work). Hear again the report of Jesus ﷺ in his Sermon on the Mount:

> Blessed are the poor in spirit, for theirs is the Kingdom of Heaven.
> Blessed are those who mourn, for they will be comforted.
> Blessed are the meek, for they will inherit the earth.

Blessed are those who hunger and thirst for righteousness,
    for they will be filled.
Blessed are the merciful, for they will receive mercy.
Blessed are the pure in heart, for they will see God.

So, too, said the closest to Jesus ﷺ in the brotherhood of God's prophets, Muhammad ﷺ:

> God's Messenger ﷺ came out to us on the night of the full moon and said: "You will see your Lord on the Day of Resurrection as you see this [full moon]. Nor shall you have any difficulty in seeing Him." (*Bukhârî*, No. 7436)

For this vision we work.

2nd
MYTH

CHARITY IS NOT NATURAL TO MUSLIMS

BECAUSE ISLAM TEACHES HATE

A Solitary Rose

*I*N THE WAKE of the First Gulf War, I am hugging the men I've worked with in a refugee camp tucked into a breathtaking fold of the Zagros Mountains, the spine of the Kurdistan region. The range runs south from the borders of Russia, eastern Turkey, and northern Iraq, then southwest along the western edge of the Iranian Plateau to the Strait of Hormuz. Its melting snow streams down in glistening rivulets on an impossibly beautiful slope ablaze with little blossoms to Lake Urmia, then the world's sixth-largest saltwater lake, now shriveled to 10 percent of its former self.

It is 1991. I am 30. It is farewell.

Kurds by the hundreds of thousands teemed here months earlier, panicked by unsourced but incessant broadcasts of imminent chemical attacks like Halabja in 1988. This Kurd (I am Kurdish) strode only the University of Basel's brick and stone walkways at the time.

The sudden deluge of these refugees into Iran's northwest from Iraq near Turkey pressed the Swiss Red Cross and Caritas Europa, a European confederation of Catholic relief charities, to seek a cadre of linguists from the University. Administrators produced me, half-a-dozen translators rolled into one. Kurdish and Turkish I spoke natively. Persian and Arabic, Basel's Oriental Institute imposed. German and English came with the geography and academic air.

I'm in the throes of my goodbyes when a darting little thing intercepts my salaams and embraces. She has run to the one who funneled her a steady stash of personal confection these past three months, a connection in high places; someone to coax a laugh from, a human clasp of security, a moment's play — against the grimness of another parentless day.

She is a tent-child, a dweller of the Orphan Pavilion established by the Red Crescent for the camp children now cared for communally.

Her name is Gulşin, a black-haired beauty with big dark eyes. She's come running with a smile for all the world — like the first day I saw her, and every day after. Whenever our car pulled up, there came Gulşin, forever beaming, scampering up, as if waiting every day for our arrival. I know I waited every day to see her.

I kneel down. She's in my arms. "Gulşin, my love. You know, I'm going to go."

"Oh, but you're going to come back, right? Tomorrow?"

I am returning to Switzerland. My commission is over. I tell her no. "This time, I don't know when I'll be back."

An endless smile ends at last. A tiny face goes taut. Searching mine, her eyes try to understand. A cry wells within. Then trembling lips blurt out a thing too searing to be said: "If you go, who's going to take care of me?"

Those dark, wet eyes. That desolate look. They pierce my heart through. I have to look away. That's when it struck me. All the Gulşins of the world, what if they ask: Who will care for us?

The name Gulşin means Red Rose.

My soul stirs for a lone little flower, precious in my hands. It quietly questions me: Why do you look left and right? It says to me: Who will care for them? And then, as if in a thick whisper: Why shouldn't it be you?

God bless Gulşin (a young woman now, about the age I was then, if she lives) — Oh, for the little blossoms! — my inspiration to establish what a decade later became the Zakat Foundation.

Another Narrative

What a story I have told you about the spark that lit my way to the Zakat Foundation — *me and Red Rose, the little orphan girl, parting on the picturesque spring slopes of Lake Urmia* — and every word of it true.

But others bewitch you with a different origin story about Muslims and their institutions. They cast the spell of their narratives far more widely, elaborately, and persistently than I have mine. Theirs is the dark tale of a people disaffected with life, filled by their religion with hate for all others, concealing their malice behind facades of fellowship and fronts of goodwill.

However nice you might find your Muslim colleague or neighbor, they warn you, no matter how genuine and compassionate he or she may seem, or how much open good you may see Muslims in association do — even for you or someone you love — they can turn on you in a moment. In fact, they seek only the chance to do so, to impose themselves and their draconian religion on you — with that conjuring word, *sharia!* — because they delight in extinguishing people's freedoms, especially if you are a woman.

The moral of their story? Never trust a Muslim. They are loyal only to their own and incapable of selfless concern for the welfare of others. Their story is false.

Behold our "Second Myth" about American Muslim charities: *Charity is not natural to Muslims because Islam teaches hate.* It is also the most hurtful of our nine damaging fallacies because it is the most odious, an out-and-out libel that should need no refutation.

And yet it does. How has this come to be?

The Poison …

To contend that Islam subtracts the charitable inclination from Muslims maligns Islam as a religion. This is obvious. But it does something more. It makes it possible to dispute the continued humanity of its adherents. And while we may intuitively recognize this as bigotry when we see it in black and white, it is increasingly *the* prime integral of a rising worldview that seeks to diminish the value of our common humanity and justify all manner of new and dangerous tribalisms.

These escalating claims to special identities (which not coincidentally call ever more vociferously for the suppression of Muslims and Islam or even their elimination) come not from our natural feelings of wonder at the splendor of God: He created us all from a single male and female. Yet He made us into different peoples and ethnicities, enkindling in us a wholesome human yearning to know one another. This is, in fact, the divine purpose of earthly human difference — and the stated outlook of Islam and Muslims on humankind's diverse populations, languages, and cultures.

The new cries rallying us to group and nation — in America and Europe; in Myanmar, India, and China; even in the Middle East — are rooted in a divisive contemptuousness for others. They incite us to an unnatural abhorrence for human fellowship that ignites a contradictory and unattainable obsession with separation and domination. They inflame nothing but our lower, predatory urges, our dark attitudes of fear and hate, our base behaviors of aggression — and that is, in fact, their mercenary purpose: to shift privilege, profit, and, most of all, power to their handful of proponents.

The irony is that this parochial outlook does not abide any boundaries, geographic or genetic. When it catches on, it runs like a contagion through the veins of humankind. But to gain legitimacy among people, who left to their own have an innate affinity for one another, it first needs to target for severance the most susceptible bough on the human tree; to convince people that this limb is anomalous, alien, a bearer of bad fruit, harmful to the rest. In our time, that exposed branch is Muslims.

That is why you now commonly see Muslims being splintered from society as suspect in nearly every country of the world. They — we! — have become the essential illustration justifying this factionalizing interpretation of the human family, east and west, even in the lands where Muslims themselves form a historical majority. (Storytellers there, just like here, split away Muslims from the rest of the population with the same wedge labels of "fundamentalism," "extremism," and, of course, the *sine qua non* of all designations licensing the most savage suppression of our age, "terrorism.")

These enchanters accomplish this amputation of an astounding billion and a half people — dividing nearly a quarter of the human family from itself — by reinforcing an identification of Islam and Muslims with violence and terror. Few are the mythmakers. Yet deftly they appropriate the means to provide a near continuous feed of their divisive message

58

into virtually all channels of societal discourse and public presentation.

This convergent communal messaging in a society is called the public curriculum. It can speak truth or lie. It is the subject matter of all shared media forms — news, the arts, education, and information — aimed at inculcating in us a judgment and stance for or against things, shaping our worldview. So pervasive and dogged have been the pairings of "Islam" with "violence" and "Muslims" with "terrorism" in the American public curriculum that in our citizenry's minds these words now intuitively suggest each other, even if we know them for the deceptions they are.

The intent and the effect of pumping this disinformation into the public vortex is to create a social centrifugal force that pulls apart the natural human bonds between Muslims and the people they live with in society. One may ask: *Why have these information magicians singled out Islam and Muslims as their target?*

The answer is twofold but simple: First, despite their overwhelming numbers, Muslims make up the most widespread vulnerable cohort in the world. As a Muslim, I say this with pain. To look across the earth — especially from the humanitarian vantage — is to see just how frighteningly unprotected Muslims today are (an important point of understanding for a question to come, so hold on to it). Second, Islam alone among the world's religions and ideologies of our era remains unaltered by interpretation to concede God's sovereignty to man.

The Muslim community's weakness coupled with Islam's categorical denial of the possibility that some human beings can be superior to others render Muslims an ideal, even essential, victim of groups whose basis is the corrupted notion that something intrinsically different about them as a people separates and elevates them above everyone else in humanity.

Think about this. The validation of these self-cordoned groupings depends on infusing the human family with the poisoned logic of supremacies. What else could vindicate a random ranking of human beings and communities into what is in truth nothing but a baseless caste system?

We are not speaking of any "merit" of supportable beliefs these claimants to supremacy have. Nor do their actions corroborate the superiority they espouse for themselves. They do not race one another to the good deeds of providing selfless care and illumination to others. The good acts they seemingly do give them no eminence above those they help. How could they, when these supremacists tie their "goodness" to a humanitarianism of racial condescension, political repression, economic exploitation, and sexual transactions? And where is the moral rectitude in recklessly denying the human rights of the oppressed in their own homelands in exchange for empathy? Where is the ethical virtue in rejecting the asylum of the refugee and sanctuary to the migrant in the home countries of those alleging their human ascendancy?

Will they then decry the loss of the charitable impulse in Muslims? The standard of compassion the Quran sets is that of equally created servants, all impoverished before God, helping others in need, not for worldly gain or human gratitude, but in thankfulness for the blessings of life, guidance, plenty, and promise—all received by grace, which is to say *without* merit. In contrast, the only proof of supremacy given to us by those laying claim to it is the dumb luck of congenital accidents and material accumulations. I was born in this place, to this ancestry, at this time in history, belonging to this nation, or having amassed these gains.

Yet the vague notion that biology and the past have conspired to raise the racial-cultural-societal primacy of an "exception" among humanity above all others grows (each empowered identity group slotting itself into the top echelon). And along with it swells the need to single out a counter-community, something nearly subhuman, lowered to the lees by unexceptionable reciprocal forces in the distant haze of history and evolution.

... And the Cure

This is the context of our "Second Myth" about American Muslim charities, manufactured precisely to pique American misgivings in the form of a question: *If Islam has stripped the human inclination to charity from the Muslim heart, what is the real work of American Muslim charities?*

And the sorcerers for supremacy, who have posed this question to the popular mind in the first place, have, of course, readied the "logical" arguments of its answer for a public they themselves have for decades massively emotionalized and propagandized to distrust Muslims: *Here are Muslim institutions aggregating funds mostly from a people dehumanized by their religion, irremediably maladjusted to the modern world, and part of the community that is the mainspring of the planet's increasing discord through arbitrary violence against its natural order, with us on top. They must be part of its jihad against us.*

60

It thus has become the "rational" expectation of people, and hence a central policy of power, whether written or understood, to over-scrutinize American Muslim charities to the point of paralyzing them; to disassociate from them until they become pariahs in the eyes of society's essential institutions; and to thwart even their voluntary humanitarian work in principle — especially abroad — in the name of security and national interest.

This presents a twice-detrimental paradox. First, who better to bear witness to the good will of the American people toward all — and especially to Muslims propagandized by the idea that Americans are dispositionally against Islam and Muslims — than America's Muslim charities?

Second, America's Muslim charities are often in the best position to raise funds from their donors and personally deliver help to millions of the world's afflicted because so many of them in these times are Muslims themselves: We have the networks. We speak the languages. We know the communal dynamics. We understand the religious sensibilities that move both likely donor and needful recipient.

Instead, *your* American Muslim charities — and I emphasize that we tell a quintessentially American tale — now labor under an intolerable burden of suspicion and against a building headwind of jingoism that sets the country's political will in opposition to them. Even as I write these words to break the spell that conjures this worldview, I know you can still feel its enchantment because that's how pervasive the incantations of its narrative have become.

It has but one antidote. Truth.

Islam Lived Is Charity

The truth is charity is a native human instinct, and Islam scrupulously hones it. To be raised with a sense of Islam or in a culture sprung from it, as I was, is to grow up *living* the charitable ethos.

As a child in the poor and remote Kurdish village of Surtepe in agrarian southeastern Turkey, charity was nothing I had to learn moralistically or even think about logically. Zakat, the obligatory annual poor-due, and *sadaqah* — literally 'truth-affirming' voluntary charity — formed the foundations of our modest village way of life. (See the opening story of chapter 9 for an illustration of what I mean.)

I wish in no way to convey even a semblance of cultural chauvinism, the errant sentiment that underlies this, our second fallacy. So I will explain the charitable motif running through Islam that I am talking about. Forgive me in advance for a bit of lengthiness. But you need this background to help you understand the deep wellsprings and urgency of Muslim charitable giving.

It begins, as all things Islam, with God.

Charity and Human Nature

The Quran tells us that God has kneaded charity into the human 'fitrah.' This is an Arabic word that names the "pure human nature," or "natural disposition," that our sole Creator breathed into each one of us, not just Muslims. This means we human beings come into the world, not originally sinful, but congenitally upright. ❨Very truly, We created man in the fairest stature❩ (Sûrat Al-Tîn, 95:4) — that is to say, as an honest and honorable creation. That is why charity, the love of human-kind, is literally *of* the human essence.

> ❨Set your face to the true Religion, being upright. This is the 'original nature' from God, upon which He originated all humankind. There is no altering of God's creation. That is the upright Religion, though most people know not.❩ (Sûrat Al-Rûm, 30:30)

The Quran clarifies that this "upright" human makeup is not to manifest itself only in ritual worship. ❨Righteousness in the sight of God is not the mere turning of your faces in prayer toward the East or the West.❩ The Quranic word I am translating as 'righteousness' also means 'charity' and 'charitable gift,' as it does 'piety' and 'obedience to God.' So though ❨true righteousness❩ dwells in our souls, it finds its most tangible expression in the 'piety' of ❨one❩ in obedience to God ❨who — despite his love for it — gives of his wealth in charity.❩ Nor does the Quran speak here to an undirected giving. It expressly singles out for this relief ❨close relatives in need and orphans, and the indigent and the wayfarer, and beggars, and giving for the emancipation of slaves❩ (Sûrat Al-Baqarah, 2:177).

More than 60 times the Quran explicitly bids and exhorts people to activate their charitable nature in this life (and hundreds more implicitly), linking charity emphatically to our everlasting salvation in the Afterlife, which, in significant measure, depends on it. This last point may surprise you, but charity is that crucial in Islam.

> ⁅O you who believe! Spend charitably out of what We have provided you, before a Day Hereafter comes in which there shall be no trade, nor friendship, nor intercession.⁆ (Sûrat Al-Baqarah, 2:254)

In other words, there will be no chance for us to evidence our case for God's saving grace on the Day of Judgment. The life of this world is the place for that. For though it is popularly preached in America that faith on its own can save without works, Islam has never delinked belief and deeds as a necessary fusion for human redemption. Hence, the word of faith on the lips alone is insufficient. We must bear out by our actions what our hearts really believe — and no deed testifies to the fruitfulness of one's faith like charitable giving.

> ⁅The likeness of those who spend their wealth seeking the pleasure of God — and as an affirmation of faith for themselves — is as the likeness of a garden on a hilltop struck by heavy rain, such that it brings forth its produce twofold. And even if no heavy rain strikes it, then a drizzle suffices. And God is all-seeing of all that you do.⁆ (Sûrat Al-Baqarah, 2:254)

The Quran obliges charity as a commandment from God on a par with faith itself. ⁅You shall believe in God alone and His Messenger! And you shall spend charitably out of that wealth over which He has made you trustees⁆ (Sûrat Al-Ḥadîd, 57:7). Note how in the conception Islam builds in the Muslim mind one's wealth belongs to God who gives it into our stewardship. Thus the Quran urges us to give by way of admonition bordering on a demand to do so.

And how many times does the Quran addend to these injunctions utter condemnation of those who refuse to fulfill this defining function of our creation — the human nature divinely cast into us — to give in charity! What I will cite from the Quran in this regard is heavy. Yet it comes in defense against those who defame Islam as robbing Muslims of the charitable inspiration and hence our humanity.

> ⁅Nor do they spend anything for charity without being averse to it. So let neither their wealth nor their children stir your admiration. God only intends to punish them thereby in the life of this world

and that their souls may vanish while they are disbelievers.❭ (Sûrat Al-Tawbah, 9:54-55)

❬They withhold their hands from giving due charity. They have forgotten God. So He has forgotten them. Indeed, it is the hypocrites who are the ungodly.❭ (Sûrat Al-Tawbah, 9:67)

❬And among them are those who made a covenant with God, swearing: If He gives us of His bounty, we shall most surely give charity, and we shall most surely become of the righteous! Yet when He gave them of His bounty, they became miserly with it. Then they turned away — and thus did they forsake their covenant. Thus in consequence, He has fixed hypocrisy in their hearts until the Day Hereafter when they shall meet Him, for they have failed before God in what they had promised Him and because they have been lying.❭ (Sûrat Al-Tawbah, 9:75-77)

Far from Islam extinguishing the charitable inclination in Muslims, it has rather made it the defining quality of true religion in action and a necessary habit of the heart for any who would retrieve the eminence of the innocent goodness with which God originally created the human being. As these verses have illustrated, the Quran not only makes charitable giving its primary proof of the sincere religious character, but it likewise makes the refusal to give in charity its key evidence of religious hypocrisy.

Charity, a Spiritual Technology

The Quran elevates the prophets above all human beings, and Muslims hold them — each one, and undifferentiated in faith — in the highest esteem. They are God's guides and role models sent to lead humanity. The Quran particularly itemizes the poor-due as one of three essential expressions God gave to every prophet with the specific purpose of bringing to flower the charitable nature He instilled in us.

❬And We made them exemplary leaders, guiding by Our Command. For We revealed to them the doing of good works, and the establishment of the Prayer, and the giving of the Zakat poor-due.❭ (Sûrat Al-Rûm, 30:30)

This verse of the Quran verifies something else important here: Zakat almsgiving is not specific to Muslims and Islam. It formed (and forms) a rule of the essence of all the Heavenly religions. To read the Quran, to learn the elementary teachings of the Prophet Muhammad ﷺ, is to know that God loves, lauds, and adjures us to give freely and frequently from the best of what we have to those in need, even if we are in want of it ourselves. Indeed, one's goodness depends upon it.

> ❦You shall never attain to virtue until you spend in charity from that which you love. And anything you spend, indeed, God is all-knowing of it.❧ (Surat Âl ʿImrân, 3:92)

> ❦Thus they feed with food — despite their own desire for it — the indigent, and the orphan, and the captive.❧ (Sûrat Al-Insân, 76:8)

Ponder for a moment both these cases. The Quran is instructing us to give from the material wealth we have passionate attachment to, on one hand; and to feed the famished poor, the parentless child, and the detainee, on the other — even when we ourselves hunger from want of food! These divine injunctions to charity lay out for us a systematic treatment to overcome our preoccupation with the call of our own souls and to put the souls of others before our own.

The point of this charity, the verses tell us, is to "attain to virtue." (The second verse comes in the course of the description "as to the virtuous.") This makes charity a prime spiritual instrument, a sacred technology for elevating our own character to a higher moral standard. So the cry of the Quran to come to the aid of the least of us pierces all the more deeply when we realize that the needy mentioned in this second verse clearly specify categories of people facing life-and-death disasters.

I underline the condition of the afflicted whom the Quran names here because one lie currently being fanned by the dubious class of professional Islam-haters that flourish in our time is this: *The Quran teaches that Muslims must not provide relief to people because disasters are a punishment from God, and for Muslims to try to alleviate the suffering of afflicted people would be to go against God.* One weeps with the wounding of so malicious and fallacious a statement, and all the more because its reasoning — so clearly spurious as to be utter nonsense — could find so many eager to believe it about Muslims.

This is a patent libel against the Quran. Indeed, the opposite is true. The Quran records exactly the argument we've just seen attributed to

Muslims as the logic of those who deny that the Quran is Heavenly Revelation when it admonishes them to provide charitable relief to the hungry struck by disaster:

⟨Moreover, when it is said to them: Spend in charity out of what God has provided you, those who disbelieve say to those who believe: Shall we feed one whom had God so willed He could have fed. You have fallen into nothing but clear error!⟩ (Sûrat Yâ Sîn, 36:47)

We ourselves bear witness to this sentiment increasingly articulated by those whom God has empowered and enriched in our society. How often do we hear the opulent and empowered among us either blame God for not giving the impoverished provision; or blame the poor themselves for their condition; or cite the state of the destitute as a sign that God has not favored them because of sin as He has the wealthy, whose material enrichment the followers of prosperity theology hold up as proof of God's love and approval of them?

Yet wealth has no special virtue in the sight of God, the Quran tells us, except when its bearer dispenses charity from it. Then it becomes pure, and from it flows the worthiest kind of gift. The Prophet Muhammad ﷺ said: "The best charity is that which the wealthy one performs" (*Bukhârî*). That is because one blessed with much who gives it freely to the needy has transcended the greed of his or her clay nature and heeded the call of Heaven to act on the higher charitable inspiration God blew into us.

⟨So fear God as much as you can, O believers, and hear and obey. And spend charitably in what is good for your own souls. For whoever is safeguarded from the avarice of his own soul — then it is these who are the truly successful.⟩ (Sûrat Al-Taghâbun, 64:16)

In this regard, the Prophet Muhammad ﷺ said: "There is not a day wherein the servants of God awaken save two angels descend. Thereupon, the first of them says: 'O God! Give the spender in charity replenishment. Then the second of them says: 'O God! Give the miser depletion'" (*Bukhârî* and *Muslim*).

The Ends of Charity

This, then, reveals the daily mindset of the conscientious Muslim. Far from etherized to the human impulse of charity, we are literally "woke" to the crucial need to *make it happen* every living day. Long have both Muslims and external observers described Islam as a way of life. Look closer and you will see that Islam has laid that way from end to end with the paving stones of charity — a charity the mortar of which is nothing if not love.

Here, in the tenor of the Quran, rings the true call to charity that Islam teaches and God rouses Muslims and (truth told) all human beings to — its promise so thrilling it impels one to a life-purpose of giving; its qualities so fine they cannot but ennoble the human soul. But of all charity's commendable enticements, only one scales its loftiest height: The prospect of attaining God's love.

To this single vision does the Zakat Foundation aspire, the blessed end of all American Muslim charity:

> ❨And hasten to attain forgiveness from your Lord — and a Garden in Paradise, whose breadth is the heavens and the earth, prepared for the God-fearing: The ones who spend in charity, in times of prosperity and adversity alike, and who suppress their rage, and who pardon people — for God loves those who excel in doing good.❩ (Sûrat Âl ʿImrân, 3:133-34)

12,964

Americans who received mental healthcare and counseling
in 2017 through the Khalil Center,
a psychological and spiritual wellness program of
ZAKAT FOUNDATION OF AMERICA

3rd
MYTH

AMERICAN MUSLIM CHARITIES SECRETLY
WORK TO UNDERMINE AMERICA

The Presumption of Terrorism

*I*T IS THE winter after September 11, 2001. Zakat Foundation of America is just months old, a fledgling humanitarian charity in a two-room office with one, young part-time receptionist. She comes to me shaken in the late afternoon.

"A man keeps calling from out of state nonstop. He's scaring me."

The phone rings. I see the Caller ID. Same state. She looks fearful. "Okay. Don't worry. I'll take it."

"Hello."

"Terrorists! Extremists! Why are you still allowed to operate?"

No doubt about who's called.

"Listen," I tell him. "You are calling the wrong place. If you have proof of our wrongdoing, you know where to call. The FBI. Give them whatever you have, and let them do their job.

"If you don't have proof, then shame on you. With all the issues of real concern going on in the United States, you cannot find anything else to do but call this little organization, with our tiny budget, to bully a charity?"

"You Arabs! You always do bad. … " and on and on about Arabs.

I half laugh. "That shows how ignorant you are. You don't even know who we are here."

"Why? Are you not Arab?"

"And if I'm not, is that going to change your mind about us and Muslims?"

"Maybe."

"Okay. I was born in Turkey. I'm not Arab. So congratulations. What next?"

To my astonishment, he asks me in pure Turkish, *"Sen Türksün? You are Turkish?"* I say yes, and our conversation suddenly detours into Turkish.

"Nerelisiniz rica etsem? Where are you from, please?" I ask him.

"Istanbul," and he tells me his name, his district, and that he's from Istanbul's centuries-old Jewish community. I ask question after question to verify, until he gives me such detail he cannot but be telling the truth.

"Man, you really are from Turkey!"

I return to our original conversation in Turkish: "So you find this kind of time to call here, again and again, for this? You are so angry, so filled with hatred for a small community and charitable organization in the United States. It astounds me."

I say, "Ben, when you lived in Istanbul, did any Muslim Turks ever refuse to come to your store?" He kept a shop there. He tells me no.

"Did any Muslim ever try to harm you, or bother you, or harass you because you are Jewish?" He answers no.

"Did any Muslim ever refuse to be your neighbor because you are a Jew?" Again, his answer is no.

"Your community has this beautiful Synagogue in Istanbul, and you have the newspaper Shalom. After 500 years [that's when most of the Jewish immigrants came to Istanbul fleeing the Spanish Inquisition] your community still thrives there. Did you ever experience your community being intimidated for your belief?"

"No."

"Then why, for God's sake, in the middle of the United States, it seems like you have nothing else to do but call this little charity and persecute us? You want to know us? Come to Chicago. Have a cup of Turkish coffee with me, or tea."

70

He alters in an instant.

"I wish I were in your office now and that you had knocked me down on the ground. It would hurt and embarrass me less than these words you have said to me. I am so ashamed.

"Honestly, I think people like you do the work of angels. Please forgive me, if you can. I assure you, you will never again get a call from me — unless I'm coming to drink your coffee."

He invited me to his home to converse and reminisce, as his guest — over a cup of Turkish coffee. So civil.

Ben is a Zakat Foundation donor.

>~~~

The Subtext of Suspicion

You might judge Ben harshly for his impulse to bigotry. I admire him — not for his initial reaction, but for his capacity to self-correct. And you should too. Here's why.

Once Ben underwent the magical transformation that real-life human connection brings, he was able to take the measure of American Muslim charities — not from some external source of unverified opinion — but against the historical backdrop of his own experience and communal context. The change flowed naturally from the feeling that the hearts of people genuinely hold for one another — which is not mistrust, suspicion, and, therefore, contempt, as we are relentlessly scared into believing is "normal" today. It is empathy.

Our shared culture and history enabled Ben (impelled him?) to relate to me as an actual person, not a mass media creation or stereotype. Against the truth of his own experience and knowledge, the false perception of Muslims and our charities, in the form of the Zakat Foundation, dissolved. As soon as that veil of distortion fell away, Ben realized that only blind prejudice had fueled his hostility against this unquestionably vulnerable religious minority — a dangerous sensibility that had driven him to bad action. It must have frightened him once he grasped that the "Muslim mania" he had caught was nothing but a strain of the same harmful contagion that had forced his own community to flee to Turkey long ago.

But where did that virus of intolerance come from? Ben was no bigot at heart.

There is but one answer: Not from within him, but from an available cultural reservoir of biased preconceptions about Islam and Muslims, tapped by societal leaders and drip-fed into him through a toxic mix of menacing media portrayals of Muslims and poisonous comment on Islam.

Ben's jolt to sudden awareness enabled him to perceive in a moment a switch manufactured in the mind of the American public over the previous decade. As the Soviet Union crumbled in the early 1990s, a mass campaign exploited a long-held American notion of Islam as an alien civilization opposed and incompatible with human rights and plurality. It used this to steadily shift Muslims (and any who "appeared" Muslim in the popular imagination) into the vacant role of America's new central enemy.

Remember the embarrassingly jaundiced headlines: "The Muslims Are Coming! The Muslims Are Coming!" (*The National Review*'s 1990 shameful play, complete with racist-imaging of camel-riding raiders, on revolutionary American folk hero Paul Revere's famed April 18, 1775, Midnight Ride to warn of the British invasion); "The Islamic Threat" (*The Economist*, March 13, 1993); "The New Crescent of Crisis: Global Intifada" (Charles Krauthammer's January 1, 1993, *Washington Post* Op-Ed); "Seeing Green: The Red Menace is Gone. But Here's Islam" (January 26, 1996, from the vaunted *New York Times*). This pernicious substitution of Islam for communism and Muslims for Russians meant to incite precisely the rampant anger Ben had felt in order to direct that rage at Muslims and steer the people who adopted it.

I believe Ben's first perceptions of our new-sprung Muslim charity in the wake of September 11 do not significantly differ from the feelings that many Americans today still harbor about Muslim institutions, and particularly those like American Muslim charities that gather and distribute money.

We may think this distrust of Islam and Muslims flows as a "natural" result of the September 11 attacks, or acts of violence since — the latter massively and disproportionately amplified as terrorism if Muslims are involved. I say "massively" because as everyone plugged into news and the internet can see, there is an open, inveterate public offensive being waged against Islam to persuade Americans that Muslims — as ludicrous as this argument is — are out to undermine "their" country, establish

Shari'ah Law over it, force their conversion, and subjugate them to Islam's (always described as "draconian") rules.

I use "disproportionately" because if a Muslim commits an act of aggression it is reflexively classed as terrorism without thought or investigation. Yet even heinous mass killings by people of the majority population (17 students and staff killed and 17 wounded at Marjory Stoneman Douglas High School in Parkland, Florida, February 14, 2018; 26 killed and 20 wounded at the First Baptist Church in Sutherland Springs, Texas, on November 5, 2017; 59 killed and 50 wounded in Mandalay Bay, Las Vegas, Nevada, October 1, 2017; 27 killed at Sandy Hook Elementary School in Newton, Connecticut, October 21, 2012) are publicly downplayed as the outcome of individual problems of mental illness or sociopathic malcontent.

I am aware of *terrorism's* legal definition as *violence and intimidation in pursuit of political aims*. But that meaning has clearly given way to a popular and even politically correct characterization of terrorism as *violence committed by Muslims* period, regardless of the criminal perpetrators' motives, conditions, or mental states. This stands in stark contrast against the staunch policy of officials and editors to ascribe public savagery enacted by a Christian, Jew, atheist, or other to some variety of anti-social behavior — even though these acts often bear undertones of political intent that track back to ideologies or the open articulation of defined persuasions.

We cannot cure a fundamental communal misperception like this if we will not face it. The truth is that a history of laws, policies, and popularized perceptions imported to America from Europe in the conception of "the West" has always sought to "other" Islam as incompatible with American identity and the Constitution and present Muslims as an alien civilization's threat to this nation's people and society. That is why it is so easy to call up these antagonistic feelings about Muslims when some group with an agenda senses their "usefulness."

I know the idea of Americans harboring unfair opinions about people goes against our self-perception, which is good. A people should hold itself to a noble standard of human equality. That common virtue, how-ever, doesn't come without constant self-evaluation. So when it comes to Islam and Muslims in America today — with so much distortion and rancor on the wing — it is vital that we examine our beliefs about Islam and our historical estimation and interaction with Muslims.

I hope to set that context by speaking briefly to the history of Muslims in America, which I think is indispensable background.

⤙⤚

The American Muslim Context

Through Muslim Eyes

First, we should understand that nearly half the U.S.'s abducted slave peoples came from African regions with majority Muslim populations. This means that America's colonial and then national governments (and the practice of its slave masters) created a legal and communal fallacy. On one hand, they legitimized the benefit of the many Muslim men and women who literally built up the infrastructure and economy of this nation with their own hands. On the other, they rendered illegitimate the religious identity of these foundational Americans and denied their civil existence.

The empowered did this by melding Islam — the faith of these men and women — into a generalized complexion, "black," and by inventing a human division we now take for granted, "race." In so doing, they erased Islam from American history and blotted out Muslims from the original composition of American national identity. Then, with the Immigration Act of 1790 (against the vision of the founding Americans, as we shall see) and until at least 1944, the courts virtually blocked Muslims from naturalizing as American citizens (throttling Muslim immigration, as a result), treating Islam, as American legal scholar Khaled Beydoun puts it, "as an ethno-racial identity."

In reality, all this changes exactly nothing. For as the Quran tells us in its celebrated parable of truth and falsehood, likening what is false to the foam of rushing water and the slag of heated ore: ❮As for the froth, it fades away as cast scum. Yet as for that which benefits people, it remains upon the earth❯ (Sûrat Al-Raʿd, 13:17).

What stays in our case is this: Islam is undeniably part of the very root-stock of America's spiritual heritage — which makes Muslims one of the primary human wellsprings of American national identity.

These roots have only ever deepened in the 400 years since Muslims helped create America. That stream, moreover, has continued to run all

74

the stronger with about a quarter of all adult American Muslims coming originally out of other American religious communities, and with other Muslims emigrating to America from at least 50 different countries.

I am not endorsing the backward notions that longevity or numbers give some people preference over others in society, nor the benighted idea that race or ethnicity can establish a hierarchy of the "native" legitimacy of some above others. I am stating a fact. Muslims are undeniably primary characters in the American tale we all together continue to write, and Islam is a constant theme running through that story.

Yet the American Muslim community's expression of itself in society in the equal formation and free function of its institutions is not only being questioned, it is being deliberately thwarted through bureaucratic pretexts that our counterpart American religious communities — Christian, Jewish, Hindu, Buddhist — are not subjected to.

As Chapter 1 shows in detail, this is particularly true with American Muslim charitable organizations like Zakat Foundation. We seek to harness the highest human virtues of the heavenly faiths — godly injunctions plain and well-known to everyone — and team them with the best ideals of the American character with the purpose of activating these beliefs in the service of the needy at home and abroad.

Yet we face the near-constant and growing difficulty of American financial institutions disrupting our payments to aid the poor, refugee, orphan, wounded, disaster-struck, and widow — and for no other reason than we are Muslim. Still, the lives of the suffering literally depend on the timeliness of our monetary assistance, as do our agreements with suppliers of food, shippers, and healthcare providers, as well as our many humanitarian partners throughout the world.

This systemic discrimination against American Muslim charities from our own American institutions astonishes in its senselessness. It works directly against some of the most important American interests among the global populations we serve. This past year alone, American Muslim humanitarian expression through the Zakat Foundation furnished the best possible illustration of this country's claim to fairness and goodwill among Muslims and others in Syria, Iraq, Yemen, Afghanistan, and the Rohingya in Bangladesh.

We delivered American concern to African refugee girls exposed to human trafficking and abuse by supporting Kenya's award-winning humanitarian Heshima Safe House [now known as RefuSHE], which UN Special Envoy Angelina Jolie visited on World Refugee Day 2017.

We entered storm-devastated Puerto Rico as first responders with food, hygiene kits, medical services, and financial aid after Maria and brought a lengthy truck-caravan of care packages and water to Houston's deluged after Hurricane Harvey.

But if we are doubted, disrupted, and denied as Americans *because* we are Muslims, what, then, is freedom? What is the equality of men? What are unalienable rights? What is America? That is the struggle for the soul of this nation that American Muslims bring to a head.

American Intent

"American" is not a color or a faith. It is a voluntary communal identity of association between people "endowed by their Creator with certain unalienable rights" and committed to upholding those moral and legal entitlements on the basis of a divinely created human parity between us, in status and opportunity — "all men are created equal."

By what justice, then, can our citizen administrators and peers deny Muslims their enshrined place in American society — and specifically the right to exercise the great many clear injunctions in their religion to provide help, feed, and raise money for the poor (and that means the poor of all persuasions, mind you)? And who on earth would want — rather, believes they have the authority — to impede this free expression of the love of humankind?

Not the Founding Fathers of the American nation. There is clear documentary evidence that George Washington, Thomas Jefferson and others of their peers, prominent and common, explicitly meant for Muslims — worshiping in America free of mistrust and intimidation — to take a rightful part in America as these founders conceived it. This includes American Muslims organizing to fulfill the charitable prescriptions of their faith. Listen to James Hutson, Chief of the Library of Congress Manuscript Division, writing in its Information Bulletin in May 2002:

> It is clear that the Founding Fathers thought about the relationship of Islam to the new nation and were prepared to make a place for it in the republic. ... The Founders of this nation explicitly included Islam in their vision of the future of the republic. Freedom of religion, as they conceived it, encompassed it. Adherents of the faith

were … regarded as men and women who would make law-abiding, productive citizens. Far from fearing Islam, the Founders would have incorporated it into the fabric of American life.

Hutson goes on to tell us:

> That ordinary citizens shared these positive views [about Muslims] is demonstrated by a petition of a group of citizens of Chesterfield County, Va., to the state assembly, Nov. 14, 1785: "Let Jews, Mehometans [i.e. Muslims] and Christians of every denomination enjoy religious liberty … thrust them not out now by establishing the Christian religion lest thereby we become our own enemys and weaken this infant state. It is mens labour in our Manufactories, their services by sea and land that aggrandize our Country and not their creeds. Chain your citizens to the state by their Interest. Let Jews, Mehometans, and Christians of every denomination find their advantage in living under your laws."

It should surprise no one that the architects of this American nation knew of Islam and thought about Muslims as their fellow citizens. Hutson points out that John Locke had argued the same for England's Muslims nearly a hundred years earlier in his 1689 Letter on Toleration. This means that as a matter of principle, the Founders envisioned nothing else but that Muslims would and ought to be Americans if they so chose, with their religion and rights in tact.

Practically, these same leaders had great exposure to Muslims in America, as slaves, for one. And while they fatally tabled the fraught issue of that institution, they absolutely could foresee what everyone understood: Slavery would fail and these human beings would wrest their place as Americans.

Muslims, then, have long since formed a vital part of America. This means that both the original American vision and its practical reality show that no population group can claim a more organic relationship with America than the American Muslim community. (American Indians, of course, hold a unique place as a first nation.) Muslims have always composed a vital strand in America's braided community.

Two Roads Diverge

If nothing else reads clear about the fundamental twining of Muslims and America, then the American narrative of at least the last two decades should; for no other storyline has and continues to be more defining in our society or more consequential for this country than that of America's interaction with Muslims. American Muslims and their institutions have, indeed, become the great touchstone of the American ideal.

The inverse of this statement is just as true: The American ideal has become the great touchstone for American Muslims. Does it hold for us Muslims, with the untold investment of all our lives, hopes, children, and institutions? In other words, will America in the manifestation of its authorities and laws uphold "life, liberty, and the pursuit of happiness" for its Muslim citizens? Will its "government ... and ... powers ... effect their Safety and Happiness," as Jefferson struck it in the Declaration of Independence?

Or are Muslims facing the terrible start of what the Jews of Germany suffered beginning in 1933? This is neither sensationalist nor an idle thought. American Muslims discuss this question with grave fear because the parallels between these well-established, minority religious communities in their respective societies and times are too stark to ignore.

These, then, are the real questions Americans need to answer about their Muslim neighbors, not the ones that the deeply inculcated suspicion of Muslims in mainstream American society today pose, driven as they are by a hail of negative media imaging and narrative about Islam as violent and Muslims as primed by their religion for terror; and justified, as we see, through the growing, irresponsible verification of these sentiments by opportunistic political officials and public personalities.

It is frightening as a Muslim to realize that such people both know and intend what fires they stoke. Scarier still, they appear blind to the reality that in exalting themselves with lawless insolence in the land and segregating its people into factions, in order to oppress a group of them, they — and not Muslims (or the humble Muslim charities they persecute) — are the ones subverting America.

What possible interest could Muslims have in undermining the very society they and their children and grandchildren live, strive, and play in, and — in every generation since before America's inception — have dreamed in and worked to build up? Why would Muslims seek to rip

78

up the foundations of a nation they are acutely aware their spiritual and biological forebears helped lay down, literally with their lives, in the most harrowing and poignant way imaginable?

Such suspicion is utterly unfounded. This is just common sense.

As a matter of belief, Islam strictly forbids Muslims from the socially corruptive and societally destructive behaviors that do undermine nations. This holds true even if Muslims think that these actions might bring them benefit or relief. The Quran dismisses this line of thinking as caprice and warns against it because it twists the justness it calls people to. ❨So do not follow whim such that you pervert equity. For if you distort testimony or turn away from the truth, then, indeed, ever is God all-aware of all that you do.❩

The Quran holds Muslims to a high bar of detachment. They *must* support fairness — ❨be most upright in upholding justice❩. They *must* champion truth — ❨bearing witness for the sake of God alone❩. And look at how exacting is this burden of truth the Quran lays on Muslims — ❨even if it is against your own selves, or your parents, or your nearest relatives — regardless of whether one party is rich and the other is poor❩ (Sûrat Al-Nisâ', 4:135).

It further prohibits Muslims from engaging in the unbridled partisanship the brutal likes of which we now see dividing this nation. ❨Be ever upright for the sake of God, bearing witness to truth with impartial justice.❩ Nor does Islam permit Muslims to commit injustice even when society wrongs them. ❨Therefore, let not detestation for some people induce you to be unfair. Rather, be fair! For to do so is, indeed, closer to the fear of God❩ (Sûrat Al-Mâ'idah, 5:8).

Islam does not expect social equity from Muslims alone. The Quran records an open order from God to all humankind to be fair to each other, and then directly links this to moral conduct that ends in humanitarian action: ❨God commands the execution of justice among you, and the doing of good, and the giving of charity to close relatives❩ (Sûrat Al-Nahl, 16:90).

This is the essence of what the Zakat Foundation *of* America stands for *in* America — ❨the doing of good and the giving of charity❩. We see the divine decree to hand alms and aid *to close relatives* as a call to create networks of relief among the entire human family.

Far from undermining America, then, the Zakat Foundation strengthens it at home and enhances the goodwill of others toward it abroad — openly and gladly, no secret about it.

><del><</del>

A Hope and A Prayer

I told you at the outset the story of Ben, saying I admired him. For in the godly command for human beings to treat each other fairly, I see his reflection. He turned from bigotry against Muslims and suspicion about the Zakat Foundation to justice, doing good, and giving charity — exactly in the sequence the verse says we all should.

My episode with him gives me hope that when people now terrified by this wall-to-wall anti-Muslim fear-mongering personally connect with us, it will spring their natural human empathy and wash away this manufactured mistrust. The clouds of distortion will clear. The suspicion of Muslims and our charities will drain away. Then, like Ben, they will become our well-wishers and supporters of those down in the dust we are honored to serve.

In truth, I have witnessed many such changes through the walks of American life. For this, my faith that America will come to the same transformation outstrips my fear of its slide into utter darkness. For this, I pray to God that the goodness of this people will shine through.

6,924,486

Number of nutritionally complete meals for families
ZAKAT FOUNDATION OF AMERICA
procured and distributed to those in need
in America and the world from 2003-2017

4th
MYTH

ISLAM FORBIDS MUSLIMS FROM HELPING PEOPLE OF OTHER BELIEFS

To Be A Witness

*I*T'S 8 A.M. Sunday, December 26, 2004, summer's sixth day in Indonesia. A 19-inch hump wave unexpectedly raises and lowers Muhammad Nazar's fishing boat off Sumatra's Indian Ocean. About 32 nautical miles lay between him and his coastal village home of Banda Aceh to the east.

"An earthquake," he thinks, not uncommon. But while slight, the undulation beneath him somehow makes his heart "uncomfortable." He heads home.*

His heart was right.

He also guessed right about the temblor. What he didn't know was that a minute before and 155 miles south-southeast marked the ocean epicenter where the Indian tectonic plate had just smashed into the Burma plate only 18 miles under the seabed, beginning the Indian plate's 12-mile slide beneath its counterpart.

Over an 8- to 10-minute span — the longest plate incident ever re

---

* Nick Logan, "Indian Ocean Tsunami: Remembering the Day the Wave Came." *Global News*, December 25, 2015.

corded — the crash steadily unzips 745 miles of fault line northward, like ice cracking the frozen surface of a lake thelength of California. At an astonishing 1.5 miles per second, the fissure races upward passed Sumatra, India's Nicobar and Andaman Islands, and nearly into the Bay of Bengal, "upthrusting" the ocean floor all along the way to its west, and dropping it into a trench to its east.

Minutes later, the shore waters of east-lying countries like Sumatra and Thailand "inexplicably" drain away (toward the trench) exposing a great expanse of ocean floor and drawing exploring children and tourists to collect its suddenly uncovered shells and trinkets.

This hi-lo ocean floor eruption and collapse instantly creates a tsunami wave above it in its own image, like an N, which rapidly splits into two N-waves. One surges seaward toward distant India and Sri Lanka, which it will swamp in two hours. It lashes Somalia and Kenya just over seven hours later and reaches South Africa, the Atlantic, and finally the Pacific in something over half a day, raising Mexico's watermark by 8 feet.

The other wave rushes landward, locally to the Indonesian island of Sumatra, and Nazar's Banda Aceh hamlet, which it will blanket without warning in 30 minutes, then to Thailand, slamming its beaches in another hour.

The tectonic collision has unleashed a massive megathrust earthquake, the most powerful kind, measuring 9.1 to 9.3 on the 10 point Richter scale, the fourth-biggest ever recorded. Discharging an incomprehensible explosion of energy — equal to 23,000 Hiroshima-sized atomic bombs — it flings mile-wide rocks across the seabed, literally wobbles the earth on its axis, shortens the day by 2 seconds, and hurtles its waves of devastation at open ocean speeds of up to 500 miles per hour, but barely perceptible 2 feet above the water's surface.

When the slowing waves hit the sharp continental rises, and even more dramatic vertical continental slopes off the shores of the 14 countries they will thrash, they suddenly soar from 19 inches to heights of 13, 30 (in some places 100) feet, then plow as much as 1.2 miles inland, sweeping away ships, boats, piers, bridges, roads, groves, homes, and concrete buildings in their paths.

The global swathe of destruction is unfathomable: At least 227,898 dead, a third children and 45,000 more women than men. Look at the country breakdowns: Some 167,000 in Indonesia; 35,000 in Sri Lanka;

18,000 in India; and 5,300 in Thailand. Add in 5,000 tourists, many drowned in their resort hotel rooms, 543 of them Swedes (making it that nation's largest death event since 1709), and 539 Germans.

The waves injure half a million; expose up to 150,000 to deadly infectious diseases; erase 141,000 dwellings, leaving 5 million homeless or cut off from food and water. A million lose their livelihoods temporarily or permanently. As many as 1.5 million children are wounded, displaced, or orphaned.

Assistance and reconstruction will cost $7.5 billion and yield the largest humanitarian disaster relief effort in history. Zakat Foundation rallies its donors in Muslim communities across America, not just online but in person, initiating the biggest charity campaign of its then three-year existence. Its support staff speed to Indonesia, India, and Sri Lanka with disaster management expertise and donated aid to distribute.

The 2004 Tsunami is the worst ever recorded.

The phone rings in my Zakat Foundation office. A Muslim on the other end, whose observance would mark him as devout, swamps my salutations of peace in an angry wave.

"Why do you help these sinners? Do you know what goes on in Bali? Every kind of sin, fornication, immoral act, and transgression! So why are you helping people punished by God?"

I am stunned, my mind momentarily flailing. Am I hearing a practicing Muslim say he sees natural disasters as a judgment from God? Is he rebuking me for organizing the Zakat Foundation's humanitarian response to this worldwide catastrophe?

I recover, feeling a surge of my own.

"Well, my brother," I say, "if God is sending down punishment for fornication and everything else you say, then what should we think about Copenhagen, or Hamburg, or how many other western cities? What about Sao Paulo in Brazil?

"In any of these places, you can find all manner of sin. So if God will punish, why a tiny village in Sri Lanka? Why Java? Why Banda Aceh?

"In fact, most of these people were poor, pious Muslims. Why, then — if this is the logic — did the tsunami sweep their homes away, take their parents and families, drown them?

"And how can we tell what is God's punishment, and if this came as

His judgment?

"No. That is not our job, my brother. You have it wrong. God did not appoint us Muslims as judge and jury. That is Him and His. You and me, we are just His witnesses. That is our agency. And that is why we coordinate as humanitarians — to witness from the place of being human, to act from the soul of our human nature when we see someone just like us, that could be us — a human in need, aching — our witness is to intervene with help.

"Ours is not to judge others, or even to hold preconceptions about someone's suffering. Ours is to witness, which means to be conscious and then act on that consciousness in a human way.

"That is our role as humanitarians, as Muslims, the Middle Nation of compassion: To help as many human beings as we can. To save as many people as we can. To be there for the victims — victims who are crying, victims who in an instant lost their families and livelihoods, victims who are in pain.

"That's what we know God ordered us to do. That's what the Quran tells us to do. That's what the Prophet, peace be upon him, showed us to do. That's what all Islam's teachings warn us to do.

"So that means I should maybe ask of you something — to turn your thinking around. You should applaud institutions like Zakat Foundation for this relief it is arranging and delivering on behalf of the whole community because this is the responsibility of every one of us, including you.

"That's what it takes to be a good Muslim: To help others in need. To stand for them when they're struck down. To pull them up from the dust with our own hands, not asking them first: Do you believe like me? Do you look like me? Do you live like me? That's the clearest teaching of Islam — One God. One humanity.

"So no judge and no jury, brother. You are a witness. We are witnesses, asked by God to do our best to help people — all people — out of misery when misfortune falls on them, up from affliction when disaster undercuts them.

"So to answer your question, brother, Why do we help these people? Because that's Zakat Foundation's guiding principle — and it comes straight from our hearts from the heart of Islam."

The Test of Life

The incident I've just recounted took place 14 years ago; yet its insinuation disturbs me now more than when it happened. Then, a rash Muslim, out of sync with the sources of his faith, raised a wrongful judgment (with the director of a Muslim charity) and got set aright.

In the years since, a hardened cadre of antagonists to Muslims has emerged to pour their considerable money and malice into one mission: Turn people against Muslims in American society, delegitimize them, deinstitutionalize them, and, if possible, depopulate them. The Southern Poverty Law Center lists some of these individuals and their associations as hate groups. Disinformation about Islam powers their sweeping public campaign, including a direct attack on American Muslim charities that seeks to spread a gross misinterpretation similar to the caller's errant understanding; namely, that Islamic Law prohibits Muslims from helping non-Muslims because the latter are going to Hell.

This is the inverse of the truth. Even now, as I write these words, Zakat Foundation emergency aid and relief workers gather and distribute life-saving food, water, medicine, and help to the people of Indonesia's Sulawesi Island, many of them Christian, struck by a 7.5 magnitude earthquake and yet another devastating tsunami, leaving at least 1,234 dead (and likely hundreds more) and upwards of 200,000 homeless.

We do this *because* Islam commands this kind of active witness to professed belief expressed as humanitarian service to all other human beings, especially those in critical need of life-saving aid. With impassioned repetition, the Quran tells Muslims that a primary cause of human failure is our obstinate refusal to operationalize our claim of faith in One God, that is, to act in the most basic way on our humanity. In evidence of this, the Quran carries us to the Afterlife so we can hear direct human testimony from those who did not pass the test of earthly life about a main reason that they lost their souls everlastingly to the rebuke of God. Look at their answer: ⟨We were not of those who prayed. Nor did we feed the indigent⟩ (Sûrat Al-Muddaththir, 74:42-44).

Think about this. The Quran links ritual worship to charitable action that sustains the life of the poor and dispossessed. Not feeding the hungry can seem to us a small neglect for so great a forfeiture as the loss of everlasting happiness. Yet God embedded compassion for others in the human heart and then fixed this — in that same piece of flesh in our chest — to genuine belief in Him. In other words, you do not truly believe in God if you do not *succor* the vulnerable. And whoever does not *succor* the vulnerable does not truly believe in God in his or her heart, no matter what one's mouth says. I have highlighted 'succor' here, knowing this term has fallen from fashion, because it is the right word to use. It literally means to 'run up to the help of' someone, to 'rush to something or someone from below,' that is, to uphold the needful with aid when they suffer collapse from calamity.

'Succor' precisely defines the Quran's repeated description of how all the prophets of God, and the believers who followed them, fulfilled His command to act as one faith-community, and expressly in rushing to the aid of other human beings. This comes, moreover, with the specific warning, so relevant in these times, not to ⟪split into factions among themselves … each party exulting in whatever they had taken hold of⟫ and believing that something special about *them* — in creed and essential quality — makes *them* humanity's exceptional grouping.

The Quran does not allow for such identity politics when it comes to the collective human obligation to act as one in the interest of others in need. Nor does it leave unqualified the kind of unity in faith it is prescribing. It characterizes the sincere as "cautious," that is reflective, about the consequences of their actions, and explicitly about what they take in and what they deal out. Pay heed here. A person of upright faith following upon the footsteps of the prophets of God, according to the Quran, restrains him- or herself to consume only wholesome things yet goes all out, and with urgent intent and acute humility, in doing righteous deeds.

Neither are we left to speculate about the kinds of acts that qualify as virtuous. The Quran very particularly characterizes them and the motivation of the people who do them as wholly benevolent, done for the sole purpose of promoting human welfare, in love and awe of God:

> ⟪Those who give charitably all that they give, with trembling hearts, because they know they are returning to their Lord for Judgment — it is these who 'hasten to exceed one another in good works.' And they are, indeed, foremost in fulfilling them⟫ (Sûrat Al-Mu'minûn, 23:52, 60-61).

There's where the human competition lies in the eyes of God — not in racking up profit no matter who we steamroll. Not in accumulating power, influence, and admiration to ourselves. Rather, the quest for our humanity lies in the opposite of this. Who can do most in helping the needy? Who can reach the suffering with assistance first? Who can give most from their wealth and their selves, without profligacy, to uplift the destitute and deserving?

This is why Muslims give charity. We know we hold no Godly exemption from the trials we strive to alleviate in others. It could be us. It might be. Today, it often is. We seek only God's Face in giving, His forgiveness for our failings, knowing we are frail. We are the meek.

With this fear, our hearts quaver.

With this hope, our hands work.

The Hands Follow the Heart

Nowhere will you find Islam asking Muslims to scorn the needful because of their creed, or race, or human category. In no word does the Quran exhort Muslims to fetter their humanity to the faction and the group. On the contrary, it positively dissociates the charitable witness of the Muslim — which is to come to the aid of all the weak — from an idea popularized today by the American prosperity gospel; namely, that material wealth, and specifically financial success, testify to one's faith in God and His favor on that person, or the reverse, that one's poverty or insufficiency proves God's displeasure. This erroneous belief dampens the sense God made inherent in us to rescue the poor, the debilitated, the victim, the unable, and the downtrodden. It blinds us to the trial of faith to which God has put us — to aid the poor to prosperity, the stricken to facility with something of the abundance and ability God has bestowed on us — yes, as a lofting mercy, but also as a weighty test.

The Quran addresses our errant human tendency to measure the favor of God on us according to our wealth.

> ❨As to the human being, whenever his Lord tries him, such that He gives generously to him and blesses him, he says in exultation: My Lord has honored me! Yet whenever God tries him, such that He restricts for him his provision, he says in despondence: My Lord has disgraced me!❩

Is it that *God* has shamed us if He constrains our means? ❨No indeed!》 Mindfulness of the difficulties and strain on the impoverished, the debt-ridden, the helpless — that is the lesson of our own straitened circumstances. 《But you》 human beings break the covenant of God when He enriches you. You 《do not give generously to the orphan. Nor do you urge one another to feed the indigent. Moreover, you devour the inheritance of others with a devouring greed. For you love wealth with an ardent love》 (Sûrat Al-Fajr, 89:17-18).

Our relative wealth, as a person or a people — this is no sign of our goodness in the eyes of God, nor of divine disapproval. It makes us neither better nor worse than others. It is in both instances a test of faith — and of more severe consequence for the well-to-do, according to the Prophet Muhammad ﷺ. "The affluent will be the lowest on Judgment Day, save one who gave of his wealth right and left [in charity], having earned it by pure means" (Ibn Mâjah, graded authentic). The Quran so aptly calls this giving of our wealth the "steep road." Such is our uphill battle with our soul to disburden it from the materialism it prompts us to accrue and that it ardently loves — 《avarice is ever-present in the human soul》 (Sûrat Al-Nisâ', 4:128) — and that weighs it down as it contemplates ascending the moral path that will bring it close to God. In these very terms does the Quran speak of our real prosperity and failure. 《And whoever is safeguarded from the avarice of his own soul — then it is these who are the truly successful》 (Sûras Al-Ḥashr, 59:9 and Al-Taghâbun, 64:16).

We amass wealth and our reluctance to take that rising road — burdened by our accumulations — grows, though we see clearly the signs pointing to its ethical eminence. It is in us from God to recognize the two highways of right and wrong. Yet we do not want to pay the high road's toll. For this, the Quran chastises us, even while it lists for us the kinds of self-liberation from our wealth this climb takes.

> 《Yet he has not attempted the steep road. And do you realize what is the steep road? It is the freeing of a human being from bondage, or offering food on a day of starvation to an orphan who is a relative, or to an indigent person who is down in the dust — all the while, being of those who believe — and who exhort one another to patience, and who exhort one another to mercifulness.》 (Sûrat Al-Balad, 90:11-15)

90

In fact, just as the Quran brands charity the evidence of true faith, so too it shows that repulsing the vulnerable signals one's unbelief. ❮Have you seen one who belies the coming of God's Judgment? This, then, is the same one who repels the orphan and who will not urge the feeding of the indigent❯ (Sûrat Al-Mâ'ûn, 107:1-3).

Yet look at the Quran's startling conclusion after these verses. It issues stern warning — *not to the unbelievers* — but to those who, in body, offer ritual worship purporting belief, but whom it labels "unmindful" of the meaning of their devotions! For the religious observance of the heart cannot hold true, the Quran tells us, if it fails to activate one's hands in securing comfort for the afflicted and the necessities of life for the needful. ❮So woe to all those who pray — those who are unmindful about their Prayers, those who only make a show of worship, while they withhold basic aid from others❯.

⟡

Not in text or precept does Islam constrain its people to help only Muslims. Rather, it exhorts us to just the opposite. It demands Muslims prove the truth of the faith they claim and the sincerity of the worship they perform by helping *all* in need — animal, vegetable, and mineral — but especially the people it strikingly categorizes as suffering debilitating deprivation, disaster, or societal vulnerability. And this it does with no reference to space or race. In other words, Islam identifies belief itself by the *witness* of our humanitarian action. That action's prerequisite is detachment from want of favor or thanks. Without this purely human act of pure kindness, one's profession of faith in One God hangs empty. For Islam refuses to uncouple its twin integrals of 'imân wa ʿamal,' faith and works, the paired fulcrum upon which this religion pivots.

I remind you of my statement in Chapter 2, that charity validates one's faith in Islam, the literal meaning of 'ṣadaqah,' or "truth-affirming" voluntary charity. To *be* Muslim *is* to give charity.

In this, we seek to mirror a Loving-kind God — ❮both His Hands are stretched out wide. He dispenses His ever-flowing blessings as He so wills❯ (Sûrat Al-Mâ'idah, 5:64) — unchained by the words, whims, and margins of much-bordered minds.

600,000

Minimum number of people
ZAKAT FOUNDATION OF AMERICA
has given on-demand access to potable water
through its World Well & Hand Pump Installation Program

5th
MYTH

American Muslim Charities
Foment Sectarianism

The Man on the Toppled Roof

*I*T'S THURSDAY NIGHT, December 25, 2003. I'm sitting with two friends in the tiny Zakat Foundation office near Chicago. We're a two-year-old, fledgling charity, still learning and establishing ourselves in a fearful climate for Muslims in the wake of September 11, and with little experience among American Muslims in international charitable work.

A shallow, 6.6 magnitude earthquake has just convulsed the Kerman province of southeastern Iran (there it's dawn on the 26th). Its epicenter lies just 6 miles southwest of the ancient, mud-brick capital of Bam, once a thriving trading hub along the celebrated Silk Road, home now to 90,000 mostly dozing dwellers. Just half that distance away sleeps its smaller sister-city of Baravat. Tiny villages dot the nearby slopes and valleys. Frequent tremors undulate beneath the region's mountain roots but rarely reach into the city, and even at this intensity cause comparatively little damage.

Not so this temblor. It rips through Bam, delivering devastation to 142,000 inhabitants along the deadly spokes of a 10-mile radius around it. At least 29 major aftershocks rock the region, as if heralding the world's ending to its inhabitants.

The disproportionate and unexpectedly catastrophic devastation baffles seismologists, who later detect the hidden finger of death, the previously unperceived Arg-e-Bam fault, whose rough-edged rupture line cuts directly through the city's east, where the greatest damage occurs.

The quake kills a staggering 26,271 people — Iran's greatest disaster toll ever — 11,000 of them school children and 1,200 teachers. That's nearly a fifth of the locality's 5,400 educators, debilitating the school system and "morally devastating" and psychologically traumatizing a close learning community, says its administrative head.

Researchers later surmise the horrific end of half the dead. Seismic waves shake down mud walls unfit to hold up heavy roofs that collapse, crushing people, most in their beds. Few homemade houses hewed to earthquake building codes enshrined in law in 1989.

On average, people lie alive beneath blankets of stifling rubble for nearly two hours. They suffocate to death in the enveloping pall of mud and dust that leaves few air pockets. It compresses limbs and torsos, compartmentalizing (cutting) circulation. Kidneys fail. Multiple bone fractures shred nerves to demise.

More than 30,000 suffer serious injury. In seconds, the earth-spasm erases as much as 90 percent of all Bam's public buildings and facilities — hospitals, schools, businesses, municipal structures, roads, water, waste-disposal, gas and electric systems. Gone.

It utterly demolishes three-quarters of all Bam's housing, leveling up to 90 percent of its neighborhoods, expunging landmarks and mile-stones. Bam is blotted out: from city to unmapped no man's land at daybreak. In Baravat, not a single dwelling remains standing for more than 15,000 residents.

The cataclysm instantly makes 115,000 survivors homeless — in bone-chilling December, a cause of more death. They cluster first in tents, no warmth or winter clothing. Relief workers eventually set up heated camps on the city outskirts then relocate thousands.

The Bam Citadel — World Heritage Site, Earth's largest and best-pre-served adobe structure, source of a flourishing tourism — stood watch over its city since 579 BC, 2,582 years ... turned half to dust in seconds in the Bam earthquake of 2003.

94

Days later, after offering congregational prayer in the mosque, a man speaks to me about Bam: "Listen, Bam is Shia, anyway — heretics, innovating in religion. They do ... and say ... and believe ... God's punishment ..."

His words shatter into muffled sounds and fragments against my sorrow. Before me, I see only a man, crumpled on the roof of his toppled house, amid a sea of rubble.

Beneath him, in his one-time home, lie his wife, his children, parents he cared for, relatives, entombed in the mud ruins of a perished, cherished joy — snatched away in the blink of an eye. Laughter. Love. Struggle. His life!

Deleted at dawn.

He had emerged from the earthquake alone.

When our relief team came upon him, the report said, he seemed already on the threshold of the next life. There he sat. Weeping. Weeping. He had cried continuously for days. He was still crying when they found him, without tears. He had none left to give.

Through the shivering winter days he wept. Through the biting cold nights he wept, in tattered clothes, oblivious to his condition and everything around him. His shock. His pain. His profound anguish. Desolation smothered his senses.

He had eaten nothing. He had drunk nothing. God alone knows if he slept or moved.

We tried to give him water. We tried to console him. We tried to warm him, to sustain him, to save him ... for hours. But there he sat, whelmed by his grief, his apocalyptic loss.

"These people, leave them to God's punishment. Anyway — " Words of oblivion from the yammering man in the mosque broke through.

"Do you know what you are saying?"

I buried him mid-sentence with the calamity of the man on the toppled roof. I shook the ground beneath his feet with the man's throbbing heartache. I laid waste to his thoughtless, senseless chatter with the deadening, dumbfounding agony that all this man's life had suddenly come crashing, crushing down to — in just a heartbeat.

"So now we come to it. And we claim to be Muslims, followers of

Muhammad ﷺ?

"So tell me, what do you think the Prophet of Islam ﷺ would do if he saw this man. His family destroyed. His wife and all his children dead and unreachable, beyond the *barzakh* (death's barrier), suffocated below him.

"There he sits — on the roof of his ruined house, his destroyed dreams, his desolate destiny. Sobbing. Crying in pain. Forgetting to eat. Forgetting to drink. Even to survive!

"Do you think the Prophet of Islam ﷺ — the gentlest of creation, the mercy to the worlds — is going to interrogate him about his faith if he came upon him? 'Are you Shia? Are you a Christian? Are you a Jew? Are you a Buddhist? Are you an atheist?'

"Or is the Prophet of Islam ﷺ — the one God called ❨a luminous beacon to all nations❩ (Sûrat Al-Aḥzâb, 33:46) — going to do his best to give him kindness, to show him love, to comfort him with compassion, to extend his hand in mercy, to embrace him, to hug him?"

"Yes."

"Then that is exactly what we did. And that is exactly what we will do, *insha'Allah*, whenever we can be there for people whom God has tried."

To Be Human

I meant what I said then. It means more to me now. To give of oneself *at* and *for* God's pleasure — no mustard-seed weight of judgment on the suffering, no want of reward but from God — *this* is charity as lived by the prophets — Abraham, Moses, Jesus ﷺ, and the rest, the true exemplars of humankind, whose footsteps God meant for us to walk in.

> ❨And We made them exemplary leaders, guiding by Our command, for We revealed to them the doing of good works, and the establishment of the Prayer, and the giving of the Zakât-Charity — and to Us alone were they ever worshipful.❩ (Sûrat Al-Anbiyâ', 21:73)

The Quran records the last of these prophets, Muhammad ﷺ, as the embodiment of this perfected state of "humanity" — not unattainably, as a prophet, but eminently imitable as a believing man. For that is the moral point of prophethood in Islam. It is placed among mortals so ordinary people can follow. That model (and Islam's message) is this: *With all your clay frailty, you human beings have what it takes inside you to rise up to the intended stature of your believing, benevolent humanness. (see Sûrat Al-Tîn, 95)*

96

In other words, "humanness" in the Quran is simultaneously synonymous with both faith and philanthropy. In the logic of Islam, to be truly human is to believe, and to believe is to give charity. So to be human is to give charity. One cannot be without the other.

There is not the width of a hairline between this meaning of 'human,' as the Quran reveals it, and what we know 'human' also signifies in English, as derived from Old French and Latin: "to show benevolence and compassion."

The Arabic word the Quran uses for 'man,' as in "human being," is '*insân*,' which in another likely original sense, means "to forget much," for this failing of remembrance highly characterizes man. He forgets many things, and what he is, ironically, most apt to forget is his own humanity — in both the sense that he is no more than this, a human being, and that others are no less so. They, too, are human.

Our forgetful natures call for our vigilance, lest our convictions and passions turn malignant. The Quran specifically warns us against the mutation of these moral sensibilities into dogmatism and partisanship, diseases of the mind that spread with abrupt and shattering consequence through the human community ❨who split into factions among themselves❩.

Subtle substitutes for faith and action, these two sicknesses of the human soul work in tandem in a cycling pattern of thought and conduct: "I am right, others wrong. Justly, I undermine them." Nothing hardens the human heart like acting on misbelief … until, in its factional elation — ❨each party exulting in whatever they had taken hold of❩ (Sûrat Al-Mu'minûn, 23:53) — the heart loses the limpid clarity God gave it to discern moral rectitude and awaken the deeds of virtue that uphold it, charity headlining this list of good works.

For the Quran identifies not the brain but that sentient flesh in the chest (the *fu'âd* in its Arabic) as the sensory organ by which people understand. ❨Yet He made for you the faculties of hearing, and sight, and hearts that comprehend❩ (Sûrat Al-Naḥl, 16:78). When our persuasions and preoccupations slip from belief to belligerence, hostility infuses deep into our hearts and they dim into sightlessness. ❨For it is not the eyes that become blind but the hearts within the chests that go blind❩ (Sûrat Al-Hajj, 22:46).

Dogmatism will kill truth, if permitted. In its absence, the spirit (*rûḥ*)

97

of humanity withers in us, no matter which side of this equation of utter loss we write ourselves into, empowered or powerless. It is this that George Orwell asked us to envision in *1984*, though it seems a thought experiment in language no more.

Partisanship, by nature, travesties justice, without which no social group, from family to humanity, can survive. With apologies to the Beatles, if you want to live (and love!) free in a truly civil society, all you need is *justice*.

None of us holds immunity to these disorders, but they present with classic symptoms that allow us to diagnose ourselves. We stop listening to others we see as unlike us, especially when they explode our narratives of ascension with a history of the humanity we trampled in our rise.

We cease thinking about what "others" say and dismiss their calls for consideration as protest masking (inherent) mediocrity and their indolence in self-correction. They can never become us, such errant thinking goes, but they should at least affirm our special excellence by trying.

We disallow ourselves from feeling the hardships others endure, and grow, as the old song goes, "comfortably numb" to their suffering, which we hold up as proof of their misguided disagreement with us and their disfavored difference.

Yet these selfsame signs that we have fallen into dogmatic partisanship (which we experience as our exceptional human worth) render us vulnerable to the lowly common denominator of susceptibility to received opinion and perception. Popular impression supplants our independent thinking. Our vision narrows and goes white. We search neither our souls nor our convictions anymore against some credible touchstone. Judgment petrifies into incontrovertible "truth" that is nothing but distortion. We think no more. Hearts turn to stone. Our humanity goes cold.

This makes us forget our inherent human allegiance to all others, whom we no longer fully see as people. We have lost sight of the foundations for the emotions that fired our search for a morality of reason and guidance to begin with. Far back in our memory, what was it? Oh yes. A desire to do good in life …

… And help people.

In the Footsteps of the Prophet ﷺ

When I recalled to that fellow at the mosque the habits of the prophetic heart toward the distressed, I knew before I spoke this was checkmate. Yet I did not want to speak to his forgetfulness of this (which for a Muslim of even minimal conscientiousness is a major shortcoming) before reminding myself (and you) how easily we too may slide from high-minded striving into base dogmatic partisanship.

This has one cause: failure to remain a thinking believer. God gave us minds for the express purpose of equipping us to distinguish truth from falsehood, right from wrong, so that we will *act on* that belief with self-sacrificing goodness. In the belief the Quran builds, that charitable action warrants no sense of "condescension" on the part of its doer. Any favor you confer by fulfilling the God-given human right of another in want or tribulation you do only upon yourself.

> ❧And whatever good you spend charitably, it is for the good of your own souls. So whatever you spend in charity, do so seeking only the Face of God. Thus whatever good you spend shall be rendered to you in full — and never shall you be wronged in the least.❧ (Sûrat Al-Baqarah, 2:272)

Belief binds one to the duty of that charity, which one neglects at the risk of hypocrisy, the fatal fear of the truly faithful.

This is not the intellectualizing of a modern Muslim or a religious afterthought. Exertion of one's independent understanding to translate belief into behavior forms a major theme of the Quran, and not incidentally. In dozens of contexts, its verses directly exhort people to "understand," "think," "reflect," "be (or become) mindful" — that is, to conscious awareness of their tremendous moral burden as human beings. Muslims commonly know this.

Islam inextricably links belief to thought and then, vitally, to the practical outcomes such belief entails, which the Quran almost invariably attaches to helping people — again, as an attestation to faith — in all their many expressions of human needfulness.

This brings up another essential definition of humanity in the Quran: Poverty is humankind's inescapable state, for the human being has nothing but what he or she is given — moment by moment — and not because we are deserving. ❧O humankind! It is you who are the poor, utterly in need of God. And it is God alone who is the Self-Sufficient, the All-Praised (Sûrat Fâṭir, 35:15).

Only the telltale human fault of shortsightedness keeps us from seeing the tenuous reality that separates our *sufficed* needs from the privations of the tried God calls on us to satisfy. This divine summons to enrich the poor and assist the stricken through charitable giving of wealth and self asks us to testify to the sincerity of our witness to faith by carrying out its moral imperative in the world, demonstrating we get the chain of *thought, belief,* (charitable) *implementation.* The Quran lays this down as a tangible metric of our gratefulness to God for all He provides and promises us.

All this underscores the pivotal position mental acuity holds in putting belief into practice. We depend on it to navigate life's hazards. Thus the Prophet ﷺ prayed: "O God! Show us the truth as true, and grant us to follow it. And show us falsehood as false, and grant us to shun it" (Ibn Kathîr, on 2:213). Ponder for a moment what this incisive supplication seeks: to save the mind from closure and the ensuing confusion that may cause one to misapply belief and go astray, which is precisely what the cyclical pattern of dogmatic thought and partisan conduct does.

The man who spoke to me in the mosque had become content to let sectarian *doublethink* intervene between his belief and his heart. "Doublethink," Orwell tells us, lets a person accept two contradicting beliefs at the same time, usually as a result of indoctrination. In other words, he knew very well the tenderhearted mercy the Prophet ﷺ — a double orphan himself — unfailingly showed the vulnerable. He had to have heard how particularly the Prophet ﷺ exhorted his Companions to act likewise in the selfless service of an exhaustive list of the materially, psychologically, and circumstantially needy.

Yet sectarian partisanship crept past his inattentive mind, deadening his natural human empathy for the heartrending suffering of the people of Bam. He had lost an important part of the conscious humanity his religion came to sharpen and his Messenger ﷺ arrived to epitomize. Indeed, the Prophet ﷺ himself summed up his entire call as a mission to refining for humanity its humane disposition: "I have been sent solely to perfect righteous character" (Tirmidhî).

In this light it is unsurprising that the renown of the Prophet Muhammad ﷺ with those he moved among inhered distinctly in his widely esteemed character of lenity, gentleness, care, helpfulness, trustworthiness, and generosity — even among his inveterate enemies, who history records saying as much. The Quran deeply ingrains this understanding of the Prophet ﷺ as charity's essence in any Muslim of minimal conscientiousness.

◆For We have sent you, O Prophet, as none other than a mercy to all the people of the world.◆ (Surat Al-Anbiyâ', 21:107)

◆Truly, a Messenger has come to you from among yourselves — one upon whom it weighs heavily that you should suffer, who is solicitous about you and your welfare, whose very nature … is sheer kindness and mercy.◆ (Sûrat Al-Tawbah, 9:128)

So mercy to the needful, solicitousness for the suffering — these qualities characterize the Prophet ﷺ, who nowhere justifies any semblance of dogmatic partisanship. On the contrary, the Book his prayer, his worship, his life and his death embodies requires that we ◆hold fast to the rope of God — all of you together◆, even as it commands that ◆you shall not divide◆.

Feckless calls to sectarian, ethnic, and national division (now rampant) beckon us to move away from our common humanity and incite us to conflict. Yet the Quran calls us to gratitude in fraternity and the peace it brings. ◆And remember with reverence the grace of God upon you when you were enemies and He bound your hearts together, so that you became — by His grace — brothers to one another.◆

It rallies us to ◆let there be of you one united community◆ — not docile in the face of human hardship and victimization, but standing forth ◆for the good of humankind, calling to all that is good and enjoining what is right and forbidding what is wrong◆.

It asks us to alter our worldly definitions of the "prosperous" from people who live to accumulate the things of the world, to those who selflessly distribute of the world for the sake of God so that the shamefully soaring number of suffering, wronged, and persecuted may live. Such are the humane ones working unsung to feed the starving, house the orphan, settle the refugee, heal war's guiltless wounded, and treat its countless diseased. These are the gallant, silent about their heroism. Yet their voices echo in valor from the mountains like David's, hymning truth from the mouths of those rendered mute by unutterable tragedy. ◆It is *these* who are the truly successful◆(Sûrat Âl ʿImrân, 3:103-04).

101

It is not in the direction of the false unity of the monolith — uniformity out of endless division and separation — that the Quran and its Messenger ﷺ point us to, but to the miracle of our plurality. The small mind experiences this bewildering difference as alienation. But not the eyes that see it through the Quran and the way of its Prophet ﷺ. They behold the beauty of our One God's greatness.

> ﴾And of His wondrous signs is the creation of the heavens and the earth and the variety of your tongues and your colors. Indeed, in this there are sure signs for a people of knowledge.﴿ (Sûrat Al-Rûm, 30:22)

The myth that American Muslim charities help only people who believe in Islam the way their organizers do, and so foster sectarian conflict, contradicts the spirit *and* the letter of the message we strive to uphold. Give ear to the Prophet ﷺ himself on this:

> The doors of goodness are many. … Enjoining good. Forbidding evil. Removing harm from the road. Listening to the deaf. Leading the blind. Guiding one to the object of his or her need. Rushing by the power of one's own legs to one in sorrow who asks for help. Supporting the feeble with the strength of one's own arms. *All of these are charity enjoined upon you.* (Ibn Ḥibbân)

You see this instruction for yourself. It contains no hint of partiality, pairing only deed to need. You've read how Zakat Foundation relief providers responded for this American Muslim charity to the Bam earthquake, and my withering answer to the man who questioned it on the unfounded basis of doctrinal adherence (God accept his repentance).

This understanding of how *charity* should govern the temperament and behavior of a person or an institution engaged in administering it, especially when they claim a purpose of godliness, is not special to Muslims. God has stitched its awareness into the fabric of our native human disposition; namely, that those who help others in need should do so with only His higher love as their motive, protecting *themselves* from contempt and judgment.

Such is charity's true ethic, borne down through the generations and Heavenly Revelations by all the prophets, upon whose traces Zakat Foundation directors, staff, and volunteers seek to walk as humanitarians

— promoters of *human* welfare.

From the same seed of 'increase' (one of the denotative meanings of the Arabic word '*zakât*') that the prophets planted, we have sprung and nurtured the Zakat Foundation — and ever does it remain the touchstone by which we test our performance, the ideal we attain to in our service, and the hand of loving-kindness we hold out *to all*.

6th
MYTH

AMERICAN MUSLIM CHARITIES

AID ONLY ETHNIC MINORITIES AT HOME

The Meeting

BY SUNSET AUGUST 31, 2017 — the evening start of Eid Al-Adha, the big Hajj-season holiday — Hurricane Harvey had dropped a 27-trillion-gallon lake on Texas, a year's worth of rain in five days, drowning Houston and completely flooding a third of its metropolitan area. The water weight sunk the city nearly an inch into the earth and turned the material lives of its residents into an estimated 8 million cubic yards of garbage, enough to cover more than 3,750 continuous football fields. Some 10,000 people needed dramatic rescue by first responders. Another 30,000 fled their homes in desperate search of shelter — with nothing.

Four days of Eid celebrations would have to wait for Zakat Foundation staff. Not only did we need emergency procurements of drinking water, storable groceries, first-aid supplies, hygiene products, and other life essentials, we had to stage our own football field of palletized relief provisions in Zakat Foundation's Bridgeview, Illinois, headquarters parking lot; sort the goods and pack the boxes; rent and ready the moving trucks; and find volunteers willing to load it all up after dawn prayers, truck it down, freight-heavy, at 50 mph, all the way to Houston, then hand-deliver everything to the afflicted. On top of that, it would take 24 hours of driving just to get there.

We called it the "Caravan of Love."

Turns out, it became just this, in a way I couldn't foresee.

For me, it started out as the Caravan of — What? Come On! Or maybe: the Caravan of Exasperation.

Our teams didn't suffer anything like the losses of the people of Houston — their third 500-year flood in three years — "Either we're free and clear for the next 1,500 years or something has seriously changed," as Judge Ed Emmet, the Executive of Harris County that enfolds Houston, told a *New York Times* reporter. But I felt a fierce moral duty for the Zakat Foundation of America to deliver on both halves of its name to Houston's deluged. The Quran lays special obligation on Muslims to be charitable to ❧the neighbor who is near and to the neighbor who is distant❧ (Sûrat Al-Nisâ', 4:36), especially in their time of distress. With plenty of Zakat Foundation donors in Texas, and on behalf of Muslims across America, I saw Houstonians as meeting the criteria of deserving our help and kindness on both counts.

Loading and departure day dawned. I couldn't believe what I saw before me.

A little background first. Zakat Foundation has cared for the impoverished, persecuted, and banished Rohingya people of Myanmar almost since our inception — long before the last egregious episode of their ethnic cleansing by the Burmese army, and at the hands of stoked Buddhist vigilantes, shocked the world (starting, incidentally, at the exact same time as Harvey). In fact, God blessed us to help settle one of the largest Rohingya refugee communities in the United States in Chicago's West Rodgers Park, where our supporters built the Rohingya Culture Center just the year before, in 2016, and which they continue to fund.

So, pressed to get our critical relief supplies on the trucks and down to Houston right away, I called the Center and asked them to send me a few hardy young people who could help us load, drive, and distribute the care packages when we got there.

Yet when I arrived at our makeshift loading dock, what did I see? An old Rohingya man — at least 80 — standing amid the boxes. To be sure, a couple strapping Rohingya lads had come as well. But there he stood, this elder uncle, in the rising heat. The rest of us clad in jeans,

106

T-shirts, and baseball caps (me in my work khakis), he stood resplendent in a three-piece suit — and with a fur hat atop his gray head! In the late summer heat! And we're headed to sweltering Upper Gulf Coast Texas!

In my mental state of urgent haste to get things loaded and delivered to Houston's stricken, I looked at this aged gentleman and nearly jumped with both feet in the air and screamed: What is this? I asked for strong, healthy young people to load trucks! Why this uncle? All due respect. But I don't understand.

It's not that I minded specifically, you understand. But I didn't know what to do. Uncle doesn't have a driver's license. Uncle doesn't speak English. I have no means to send him home. Nor can I spare one of the young Rohingya men to cart him back, all the way north across the city. It's Sunday, and we absolutely have to leave — and I need the young muscle and enthusiasm.

What choice did I have? I decided to take him with us, though I wasn't happy about it.

A full day's drive later, we arrive in Houston. It's a total mess. Roads blocked. No gas. No transport. We identified the central distribution hub for drop off, deep in the city center, and went there. The Muslim community in Houston — its mosques and centers — has always had admirable connection and integration of institutions. Its members used this organizational cohesion during the Harvey crisis commendably and benevolently, opening all their serviceable sites to shelter and feed the homeless. It made you feel good as an American Muslim to see the people serving their neighbors — food, water, bedding — and cheerfully, with no motive but God's pleasure. Textbook charity.

We informed our local contacts of our arrival to coordinate distribution with them. They told us that, in fact, many victims — stranded in their homes, who could not or would not leave them — desperately needed food, water, and supplies. They lived mostly in outlying areas far from the designated distribution site and had not received aid. With the help of city officials and relief workers, we pinpointed dozens of key locations and safe routes to them and began an intensive day of driving and distribution to hundreds of the unreached.

At day's end, the very last locality happened to be a small Houston Rohingya community center in a poor neighborhood ravaged by Harvey. People had left their homes and gathered in the center.

All day, we had worked at fever pitch delivering packages to those who had lost everything. The continuous logistics of driving, unloading, coordinating, and handing out had fully possessed me. (And I already have this indelible habit of working fast, running, orchestrating, which I can't break.) So I'm feeling guilty that I haven't had time to look after the old uncle. My upbringing has deeply ingrained in me this sense of responsibility toward the elderly. Tremendous qualms of conscience are panging away inside me because I'm distracted from him.

And he is helping, mind you. Here's this aged refugee, handing out one box at a time with us to people in need. You can read the happiness in his eyes, the chance to help others. He knows what it means to be driven out of his home. He knows what it means to be stripped destitute, penniless, with nothing, in need of everything, to live life at the mercy of others. What a beautiful thing it was to behold. This elderly exile, grateful to give back to the people now homeless who had graciously given him a new home, a fresh start, a sense of settled safety. You could just feel his gratitude radiating.

In the midst of my working distraction, my conscience would re-call me now and then, and I'd look around to find him, then feel sorry because there he is — suit, tie, and winter hat — in the sultry Texas weather doing his best. In the middle of that last distribution frenzy, something suddenly pulls at me: Where is uncle?

He is standing still, looking toward the community center building. I follow his gaze. There stands a man of like age. They are paused, staring at one another. The next instant, they rush to each other, and then into each other's full embrace. They weep. They hug. They kiss. They utter through broken voices words unknown, but that I can feel, of deep affection and tenderness, some deeply sorrowful happiness. They hold each other in grateful devotion, tears and words streaming. I ask one of the young Rohingya to interpret the scene for me.

The two old men were boyhood neighbors and best friends in their Burmese village. One day, in their youth, the Myanmar army came un-expectedly in the night, set fire to their village, shot people dead as they emerged from the flames, putting the villagers to chaotic flight.

The boys trekked through jungle, waded rivers, walked hundreds of miles, their families and worlds swept away in a moment, in a different kind of flood. Both eventually ended up stateless refugees in Malaysia but shunted to different camps in a foreign land, where they lost touch with one another, never knowing what became of the other, or how even to find out. (Oh for the plight of the Rohingya!)

A handful of years before Harvey, the U.S. granted both men, now old, asylum, neither one knowing of the other's providence, two of only several thousand Rohingya refugees out of 2 million to receive American sanctuary.

Here, a half-century and more later, God had decreed their meeting — a script no other could have written, with a bit part played by one too small, too nearsighted, too impatient, too insignificant to understand the plan of the Divine. Yet with all his limits, frustrations, preoccupations and shortcomings, he finds nonetheless that the All-Merciful has still favored him with the honor of driving an elderly man with a single suit and winter hat on a hot summer's day to his rendezvous of reforged fellowship 10,000 miles away.

How grateful I am for the blessing of delivering help to my brothers and sisters in Houston inundated by Hurricane Harvey — yet evermore humbled to be my noble elder's vehicle to reunion, restoration, and re-pair.

Caravan of Love, indeed.

This story has a postscript. Our elder hero and I, his faithful sidekick, have grown fast in friendship. First, people at the Rohingya Culture Center later told me the reason he wore a suit for our working road trip. When my request for help went out to Center members, uncle heard my call and resolved to help me. He had seen me many times at the Center for events — always in a suit — and his heart opened to me. He wanted to answer my call and felt he could meet me, out of respect, in no other attire.

As our attachment grew, I asked him a favor: to learn English. A companion as valuable and hardy as him, I said, would accomplish much more goodness in his new home if he could communicate with the people in their language. Zakat Foundation sponsors English as Second Language (ESL) classes at the Center. Uncle enrolled more than a year ago — and (of course, you know this) — he's in the forefront of his class.

God's ways are, indeed, mysterious.

Race as Original Sin

The preceding story exposes the flagrant (yet silly) falseness of our sixth myth: *American Muslim charities aid only ethnic minorities*. We do help Americans of smaller social groups that may suffer discrimination as a result of a difference that sets them apart from society at large (as we shall see in Chapter 7, which debunks those who try to spin this same story in reverse). Demographics and distinction, however, have nothing at all to do with giving or eliciting charity in Islam, which does not establish its standard — whether for paying obligatory alms, offering voluntary benevolence, or receiving from either — based on either population numbers or social group (though the obligatory alms of Zakat accords the local poor preference). Wealth and need comprise Islam's two main criteria for charity.

> ❰Indeed, prescribed charitable offerings are only to be given to the poor and the indigent, and to those who work on administering it, and to those whose hearts are to be reconciled, and to free those in bondage, and to the debt-ridden, and for the cause of God, and to the wayfarer. This is an obligation from God. And God is all-knowing, all-wise.❱ (Sûrat Al-Tawbah, 9:60)

So what misconception about Muslim charities does this myth really seek to propagate? One must first observe that it targets Americans who see themselves as part of the majority. When we render it legible, it says this: *Muslims won't help you in your hour of need if you're a white American because their hidden agenda aims to undermine our country's rightful majority — you — politically and socially.*

This raises the fraught question of race and America. I can sum this up no better than John Jay Chapman in his 1913 biography of the eminent (and eminently controversial) abolitionist *William Lloyd Garrison*: "There was never a moment during this time when the slavery issue was not a sleeping serpent. That issue lay coiled up under the table during the deliberations of the Constitutional Convention in 1787."

Race has roiled America from its inception and continues to do so with powerful consequence. This is not to say that the history of transatlantic slavery, or the African presence in lands that would much later become America, begins with the English narrative on this continent. Their story is their own, and actually precedes the early English influx by at least

110

a hundred years and with some "500,000 African men, women, and children who had already crossed the Atlantic against their will, aided and abetted Europeans in their endeavors, provided expertise and guidance in a range of enterprises, suffered, died, and — most importantly — endured," as William Guasco's insightful writing in *Smithsonian* reminds us (September 13, 2017).

Yet there is an important distinction to be made here. This misconception speaks to the American story of race, *not* the history of Muslim charity in America. Nor do the ideas of racial division that emerged as a 19th-century European preoccupation explain charity in Islam (as we have seen, and will briefly revisit here). Nor do these attitudes account for charity's wellspring among American Muslims and their institutional charities, which is our subject.

The American chronicle of race, moreover, is *not* remotely the narrative of race in Islam — to which I now point you. For inevitably we who compose and captain these American Muslim charities must confront the subtler and more insidiously unspoken hallucinogen of fear that this myth wants to whisper into its mainstream audience's ear: *Muslims aren't like you* — and "*like*" here means race, which this American tale has traditionally tethered to religion exclusively in its Christian dispensation.

This false logic renders Muslims perpetual aliens in America. It casts doubt on our intentions based on our religion. It disputes our capacity for altruism in the care of neighbor and nation. It underlies so much of the nameless suspicion that thwarts our genuine humanitarian work by forcing us to run a bureaucratic gauntlet of endless technicalities and procedural oppositions (see Chapter 1). It discounts everything else about us: Our heritage. Our legal rights. Our commitments. Our contributions. Our cultural experience. Our international wisdom. Our oaths. Our service. Our self-definition. In a word, it entirely *effaces* Muslims — not merely as Americans, but as human beings. Nothing short of renouncing Islam can remedy our "foreign" condition by this reasoning. Even still, the American anointing of Muslims would yet fail for those of us whom God has not made in the racial image reserved as "American" in the minds of those who equate it with white complexion.

✎

Race in the Mirror of the Quran

This looking glass of race may pervade America. Yet it remains empty of image for Muslims. It holds up no mirror in which we see ourselves or by which we see others. It has exactly zero impact on *how* we charitably deploy our persons, our wealth, and our humanitarian organizations, and no correlation with *why* we do so.

Yet the vivid way in which the Quran reflects race to Muslims has everything to do with *how*, and *why*, and to *whom* Muslims give. It shows us our own souls made luminous and transfigured by our spending of what God has freely given us, if we do this to make our faith real and with a heart longing to gaze upon the Face of God — all the while singling out none for charity for any distinction other than one's humanity, nor withholding it from any person or group. Rather, even humanness sets no limit on the charity of Muslims, for there is not an animal, plant, or any other constituent of the earth but that it has a right to our aid, our care, and our benevolence.

In this way, Islam's race narrative *colors* everything a Muslim would or could do in accordance with this religion, for we draw neither our guidance nor our sufficiency from the tints of men, but rather from ❨the hue of God alone. For who is there better than God to endue the human soul with the true hue of faith?❩ (Sûrat Al-Baqarah, 2:138). If you're looking for a theory of race in Islam, well there it is: *the color of godliness that imbues the human soul.*

As for the cause of the varied coloration of human beings, the Prophet ﷺ said: "God created Adam from a handful scooped from the whole of the earth. So the Children of Adam come forth in accord with the [variations of the] earth. So from them come the red, the white, and the black, and [those whose colors are] between these; and the soft and the rugged; and the corrupt and the good" (Tirmidhî).

He said as well: "People are the descendants of Adam, and God created Adam from dust" (Tirmidhî). And also: "There is no superiority of an Arab over a non-Arab, or of a non-Arab over an Arab, or of the red over the black, or of the black over the red" (Aḥmad).

Islam holds racism as a cardinal offense because it grows out of the deadliest sin of all, arrogance, which is, in fact, *the* original sin: that of Satan, and against none other than *us*, in the person of the father of us all, Adam, on him be peace.

112

Read for yourself:

⟨And very truly, We created you. Then We fashioned you. Then We said to the angels: Bow down before Adam. So they all bowed down, except Iblîs. He was not among those who bowed down.

God said to him: What has prevented you from bowing your face down to the ground when I commanded you? He said: I am better than him! You created me out of fire, and You created him out of mud.

God said: Descend from this blessed place! It is not for you to be arrogant in it. Be gone! You are assuredly of the eternally disgraced.⟩ (Sûrat Al-Aʿrâf, 11-13)

I am better than him. You created me out of fire, and You created him out of mud. What sentiment is this, if not unalloyed racism? So Iblîs, once of the Transcendent Assembly, begins his career disfigured into Satan, the accursed one (as a competitor to man, not to God) and as the first and foremost racist. Therefore, racism in the Quranic context is quite literally satanic. The propagation of an ideology that fractures the community of creation based upon superficial difference, aggrandizing one group over others, can only be construed as following in the footsteps of the eternally disgraced one.

Accordingly, the Quran reminds us: God ⟨*knew you full well when He produced you from the earth, and when you were fetuses in the wombs of your mothers. Therefore, you shall not proclaim the purity of your own souls*⟩ — a divine warning against arrogance. Our message: Plenty comes from God — ⟨*Then which of your Lord's bounties will you ever dispute?*⟩ (Sûrat Al-Najm, 53:32, 55) — not because of some special virtue in us.

For precisely this reason, no Muslim charity may dispose its funds — given to it to begin with out of an intention to please God by helping His creatures in need — for an ulterior motive of attaining social power, achieving political influence, in trade for another's favors, or at the price of its recipient's conversion to the giver's persuasion, or with any design on prejudicing a needful recipient. For such is not charity but bribery.

Nor may a Muslim humanitarian organization withhold relief from a soul in basic need, or threatened with ruin, or struck suddenly by calamity (particularly if it is material catastrophe), or orphaned without guardian, or stranded, or obstructed, or homeless, or displaced, or migrant, or captive, or incarcerated — especially when the wealth or volunteer action people have vested that organization with has been given to it for the purpose of replenishing those suffering these very losses.

Zakat, as an alms of poor-due, and the voluntary charity of ṣadaqah, literally aim to "purify" and "affirm" both giver and receiver. They must neither confer material profit or worldly benefit on their givers, nor undercut their recipients by bringing harm to them in any way. These purposes and limits on charity in Islam make insupportable the prospect of a Muslim charitable institution withholding it from the deprived or afflicted as a means of punishing or subduing them.

Upon this bedrock of belief American Muslims have built the Zakat Foundation of America — and these are the moral pillars that uphold it. Never would our contributors, trustees, directors or even our volunteers tolerate keeping back aid from any people in pain or privation whom we had it in our means to rescue from hardship.

Our rush to our flooded fellows in Houston (and to the similarly stricken of South Carolina before them, and Puerto Rico after, and the North Carolinians inundated by Hurricane Florence) — and all the unseen sacrifice (God sees) on the part of our staff and volunteers to make it happen, when they had plenty of excuses in reach to demur — demonstrates the sincerity of this claim. On the contrary, their reflex is ever to push us to the humanitarian forefront, in all our humble human weakness and material limitations.

And I would not have it otherwise! For I have learned at the hand of a longsuffering elder (as his personal driver to Houston) what the Quran has chanted in my heart all along.

❨Never shall God waste the reward of those who excel in doing good.❩ (Sûrat Yûsuf, 12:90)

114

89.7¢ - 94.5¢

of every donated dollar
ZAKAT FOUNDATION OF AMERICA
has received reaches the poor, and war and disaster victims

7th
MYTH

AMERICAN MUSLIM CHARITIES SLIGHT
THE VULNERABLE TO APPEASE THE POWERFUL

A New Name

*M*IGRATION STARTS THE American tale most of us live. Some have come willingly. Some reluctantly. Some in chains. We know them all and their places: Plymouth Rock. Ellis island. The nearly 36,000 voyages made by transatlantic slave ships, including La Amistad, the Lord Ligonier, the infamous Zong.*

But the first of us, these we forget — the real owners of this land, a storied people: America's indigenous.

We named ourselves Zakat Foundation of America and meant it, with the intent of distinguishing ourselves as a truly American Muslim humanitarian organization. So we purposively prefaced the story of our charity with the American Indian. An early relief specialist of ours linked us to her native Navajo nation and cleared a path for our donors' gifts to reach the people of the reservation in America's Four Corners region, where the borders of New Mexico, Arizona,

---

Voyages: The Trans-Atlantic Slave Trade Database, an indispensable, comprehensive online scholarly resource analyzing data on the slave voyages between 1515 and 1866, transforming scholarship on the slave trade.

Utah, and Colorado meet. Navajo Nation sprawls through the first three.

A year later, our colleague made a request. Go to the elders.

"They want to know you. They have questions. I answered what I could."

What kind of questions?

Who are these people that send us help?

They call themselves Muslims, after the religion they follow.

What is "Muslim"? Are they new Christians? A new religion?

No. They come originally from the Middle East.

But do they look like white people?

Yes, some of them.

White people do not give without expecting something back. What do they await from us?

Nothing. They say their religion requires them to give in kindness. They don't want anything in return.

We want to see their leader.

At the time, I worked almost alone in Zakat Foundation. I had no time to visit anyone. She persisted ... for weeks, giving me a glimpse of the Navajo will to endure. I relented.

I arrived in Navajo Nation's Arizona capital on a fall day. The Prophet ﷺ has said: "Indeed, God who is beautiful loves beauty." Undeniably, He poured no small measure of it into this place.

What breathtaking splendor! How delicate its disparate grandeur — its green valleys, stark cliffs, sudden mesas — set in jeweled relief over a canvas of endless desert. From the Muslim heart, the Quran's exclamation leaps from the lips: ❬Blessed be God, the very best of creators!❭ (Sûrat Al-Mu'minûn, 23:14).

Tsèghàhoodzàni, the Navajo call their capital, which literally translates to *Rock-with-a-Hole-Through-It*, after its most stunning topographical feature, a hollowed-out eye wreathed by the cliffs peering down at the city — and that's the first thing to know about the Navajo: the exquisite immediacy of their language seems magically to remove all intermediaries between speaker and object. They are exceptional linguists.

Navajo word meanings depend wholly on inflection, every word carrying up to four distinct meanings, each sense distinguished by its own intonation. For this reason, Navajo verb forms are especially complex. (Not for nothing did the Navajo become World War II's

118

legendary Code Talkers.)

Naming holds a solemn authority for the Navajo. (It reminds me of the Quran: ❴He taught Adam the names, all of them❵ (Sûrat Al-Baqarah, 2:21).) They tell a comical story about how they used the tonal nature of their language to alter the first appellation imposed by the American government on their capital.

They had a ceremonial name for the sweeping land tract surrounding the small would-be capital: *Ni A núgi*, or Navel of the World. And though the Navajo long hallowed this sacrosanct swath, they never settled it. In 1936, the United States Bureau of Indian Affairs commissioner made other plans. He unilaterally elected to build a capital city for the Navajo in a corner of the valley beneath the gaze of the "Perforated Rock" (the Rock-with-a-Hole-Through-It). He resolved, moreover, to focus the sacred name the Navajo used to designate the entire sweep of their holy grounds on the diminutive land patch where he aimed to set the Navajo capital. The city itself, rather than the sacred zone, would bear the untranslated Navajo name *Ni A núgi*, (inevitably Anglicized, like Chicago, maybe as Nianigi).

The Navajo objected. Shifting the spacious area's consecrated name to the narrow confines of their new little capital would diminish the sacred space's reverence, risk generational memory loss of the ancient domain's spiritual significance, and open their sanctified lands to possible future appropriation amid the emerging confusion. Like so much of their ancestral lands, the Navel of the World would vanish.

The Rock-with-a-Hole-Through-It — that seemed the natural thing to name the new capital after. Not only did the rock formation mark the precinct of *Ni A núgi*, the Navel of the World, from where their shamans retrieved water in special thread-woven jugs for ritual, but calling the city after the prominent topographical feature would preserve the broader locality's blessed identity and religious history, while giving the new city a clear-cut geographic and communal identity.

The commissioner remained heedless. So the Navajo used the only power they had in protest, their language. A slight twist of their tongues altered the name's venerable sense to the laughable mock, "Up-Your-Middle" city. Their dissent-by-lilt soon won out.

The Navajo themselves — language masters — fashioned the new capital's English name from their native epithet *Tsèghàhoodzàni* (Rock-with-a-Hole-Through-It) simply and powerfully: "Window Rock."

It lies right on the New Mexico state line atop a great uplift in the desert called Defiance Plateau (because the United States built a fort there in "Defiance" of letting the Navajo graze their animals on the rich pasturelands, and which the Navajo fought until the United States abandoned Fort Defiance during the Civil War). Four rivers cut at the Plateau's edges. Window Rock sits on the one furthest southeast, Black Creek.

From its heights, the valley seems a natural manger for it. Miles of magnificent mesas and verdant valleys cradle it. Spectacular irregular canyons that water began carving 300 million years ago in the Paleozoic Era cut through it. The majestic Chuska Mountains rise to almost 10,000 feet in its backdrop and stretch for 10 miles along its northwest horizon. Overlooking the city soars a mystic line of sandstone cliffs 200 feet high, "desert-varnished" with a thin coat of orange-brown. A splendorous patch of sky breaks brilliantly through their midst from a yawning, wind-eroded, circular arch — a "window" in the rock face, the landmark from which the Navajo Nation capital got its name.

✺

The evening after my interview with the Navajo elders, they surprise me. In the august open spaces to which they bring me, the night sky low and expansive above us, waits a teeming crowd — men, women, children — the tribe at Window Rock. There they've gathered, seated in a circle around a great blazing fire, over which slow-turned spits roast lamb and goat. (I learned then that the Navajo traditionally do not eat pork.)

It is a rite of adoption in my honor. I am deeply moved and feel undeserving.

Members garland me in succession, with a hand-woven Navajo mantle (the Navajo are esteemed for their weaving); necklaces of turquoise, beads, and stones; then gird my waist with a belt of hand-plaited leather.

An elder rises: "This our forefathers of old told our grandfathers:

'Dark days will befall our people — our lands seized, our wealth stolen. From every side will advance tests and hardship. When the shadow of these days descends, people of the spiritual world will come to you. Our prayers shall send them. They will aid you. They

120

will comfort you. Their hands will hold out to you kindness.'"

Then to me:

"You are to us of these people from the spiritual world."

I didn't know what to say. Coming from the faith tradition of the Heavenly Books — the Torah heralding the Jews, the Evangel calling forth the Christians, the Quran summoning the Muslims — we believe in angels from the spirit world. God orders them, and they come. He has assigned angels as guardians over human beings. They are our well-wishers, easing us unto good, at God's command.

How we interpret the words of the Books and prophets God formerly sent to us, and how we understand them after generations — this takes the transmission of true knowledge. But it occurs to me that the labor in benevolence we try to do — passing the provision of God onto others in need, in the likeness of His loving-kindness — this very much mirrors the work of the angels: to care for the human downtrodden, asking nothing in return. Through the eyes of Islam, I read this in the Navajo tradition.

Although we have brought them but small service, we have affirmed their humanity by acting on our own. We have accorded them the respect of fraternity in affording them what God has placed in our hands, which He alone fashioned, then opened.

But what will make us realize the desperate deprivation of the 567 American Indian tribes on their 326 often-encroached reservations? I saw living conditions on the broader Navajo preserve — home to some 200,000 people on a contiguous 27,400 square miles — that I have not beheld anywhere else in the world not besieged or bombed out: shacks for homes, doorless, with no windowpanes. Scant electricity and running water. No public transportation. The nearest store a 10-mile walk. We could not enter the home of one woman we visited because a rattlesnake blocked our way, coiled in her single room. She had no barrier to block it.

Zakat Foundation donors renovated a Navajo Community Center to enable the tribesmen, women, and children to escape the freezing winter cold and sweltering summer heat when they gathered to eat government-delivered meals, when they came.

We tried to found a vocational school: Not enough young people. Elders with no money to buy services youth might provide. Hope and a living, in short supply on the reservation, force most youth out early. We studied creating a local farming program, but the Nation's mostly older population could not sustain it.

Shunted into oblivion and mouth-taped, the dehumanization of the American Indian has never abated, their shuddering ration of wretchedness almost unrivaled by any other American racial or ethnic group.

At 26.2 percent, American Indians have the highest poverty rate of any race in the land (their own land!) — nearly double the national level — according to the U.S. Census Bureau's American Community Survey (October 2017).

Their infant mortality rate (babies who die before their first birthday) stands at 8.3 percent, about twice that of all others (exceeded only by African Americans, whose infant mortality rate stands at an alarming 11.7 percent). Native American babies die from normally treatable pneumonia and influenza four times more than non-Hispanic white babies, the standard comparative cohort, according to a 2014 Centers for Disease Control and Prevention (CDC) study of death records.

American Indian mothers die 4.5 times more often from complications in pregnancy or childbirth than non-Hispanic white mothers, reports the Center for American Progress (CAP, July 2018).

In a long-term study, the CDC found overall American Indian death rates a staggering 50 percent higher than non-Hispanic white America's. Native Americans use tobacco (and die by lung cancer) at the highest rate of any population in the country, a ratio that has lessened negligibly over time.

Native Americans experience psychological distress at double the proportion of non-Hispanic whites, with 50 percent higher suicide rates than adults of other races or ethnicities and more frequent suicides among males younger than 25, according to that same CAP July report.

And does anyone know police encounters end up killing by percentage (2.9) more American Indians than any other bracket in the country? (That's a mortality rate 12 percent higher than African Americans and three times that of whites in similar run-ins, according to the CDC.)

Native Americans have long held America's highest rate of victimization by violent crime — more than twice the national percentage — going back at least to a benchmark report by the U.S. Department of Justice released in 1999. And lest one think this violence traces back to other Native Americans, more than 70 percent of American Indian victims come at the hands of someone not of the same race.

No other American females stand a greater risk of sexual violence, a peril that has risen dramatically with the advent of the new fracking frenzy and oil and pipeline rush across American Indian lands and the ominous sprawl of their accompanying "man camps" of labor. Native American girls and women suffer rape and assault at two times the rate of women of all other races. One in three American Indian women will endure the lasting trauma of sexual attack in her lifetime, according to Canadian Métis-Algonquin filmmaker Michelle Latimer in her graphically powerful documentary *Nuuca*, a Hidatsa Indian word so heartbreakingly fitting.

It means *Take*.

Yet how generously American Indians give.

><del></del>

I am still listening at the fireside. Soon I shall break bread and feast with my welcoming Window Rock hosts. But now, the elder addressing the ceremonial gathering draws closer. He says to me in Navajo (the ceremony took place entirely in the tribal language, my colleague Franny, God bless her, translating):

"We call you our brother. We accept you into our tribe and our families as Navajo. You may dwell here with us.

"Unlike other nations, in our tradition we name people anew throughout their lives by what they do.

We name you *Niha tai hil Naha hai.**"

Brings-Kindness-with-Gifts.

><del></del>

---

* This represents the sounds to my ear. It is definitely not proper Navajo orthography. The meaning, however, is as translated to me.

Bigotry Inside Out

I promised in the preceding chapter to discredit the inverse of the myth that *American Muslim charities aid only indigent ethnic minorities*. Here we see its analog: *American Muslim charities ignore the vulnerable to win favor with the powerful*. We unmasked the former fallacy as a blatant incitement to racism — the great fault line running through American history and society. Reversing that myth's false premises does nothing to alter this judgment.

There is no need, then, to explode the present misconception by re-stating how the persistent ungodliness of racism in America perverts the context that makes so offensive an idea even viable among a civilized people; or to show again how a Muslim looking through the light of his or her primary faith-sources can only see race as a beautiful sign of the creative majesty of a singular God. Let the evidence I gave in debunking the previous fallacy — along with the testimony of our actual humani-tarian service among stricken Americans in the majority population — dismantle this counter-myth cloned in its image.

I have only one further reflection for you to consider here: the pro-phetic stance toward the humble, a fundamental moral imperative for Muslims in charitable work.

I cannot, however, forgo reminding again of something I've touched on before: these myths have makers. This should not slip from our awareness. Four generations ago, the Navajo answered the need of the day and mastered encrypting language. These times call for the converse skill: decoding the fire hose of false information drenching us every day, in this case, about Islam, Muslims, and their institutions. That means, first, reviving the will to uphold fairness for a doubted and disparaged group, then honing our ability to analyze the aims of the untruths in-vented and spread against them. If we apply this, we see the fabricators of these fictions against Muslim charities — in both the preceding mis-conception and this one — betray a singularly clear objective: Exploit America's history of racial estrangement (tied closely to religion) in order to inflame social division. That is their telltale sign. Their words seek to alienate, segregate, and disunite Americans.

But to what end?

They use these fallacies about Muslims to inject divisive enmity into society. Then they fan those volatile feelings of partisanship into "justi-

124

fiable" public actions of prejudiced intolerance. They aim to codify that prejudice against Muslims into law. (You've seen this already in feckless state legislatures barring *Shari'ah* Law and movements, especially in Europe and the Commonwealth countries, to ban Muslim women from wearing headscarves in public institutions, or even shuttering mosques.)

Where they cannot convince the courts to sanction Muslims de jure, they seek through pure propaganda to slant the social contract in order to repress Muslims de facto, to strip us of our religious freedoms and inalienable human liberties, especially our right to establish institutions. In fact, these anti-Muslim mercenaries mean to deinstitutionalize Muslims altogether.

America's Muslim charities have garnered the particular ill will of these mischief-makers because the nature of our work belies their malicious falsehoods (as you've read in the personal narratives that introduce these chapters). Still, the rising agitators of America's metastasizing anti-Muslim industry have already hoodwinked some into advancing their designs "legally," that is, through court actions, legislation, and executive decree. Even now, a robust campaign of bureaucratic attrition seriously hampers the life-saving work of American Muslim charities at home and abroad (read Chapter 1).

We may accurately dismiss the myths these purveyors of partisanship broadcast about American Muslim charities as nonsense (and most people who think critically about them do, especially if they have experience with Muslim humanitarian organizations). We can call their mechanisms for spreading these misconceptions crude (shamelessly chauvinist broadsides against Islam as a religion, xenophobic attacks on Muslims, ignorant interpretations of the Quran, vulgar representations of the Prophet ﷺ, and so on). But we can deem neither their methods nor their madness futile. The unprincipled of our world, past and present, have used precisely this technique of coupling the systematic dehumanization of the marginalized with self-flattering appeals to the supremacy of the mainstream to come to power with horrific effectiveness (yet always to a realm's ineluctable destruction). It's a simple formula: segregate the people of the land into factions. Cast suspicion on the most susceptible social group. Then use the established group to oppress them.

The demagogues who propagate these falsehoods against American Muslims and our institutions — behind the guise of suspect patriotism

— display exactly this cunning and ill intent. From the account of the Navajo, we should learn the crucial importance of calling things by their proper titles. "Treachery," I name these people. For while American Muslims and our organizations may bear the first sting and venom of their poisoned darts, if you follow their sights you will see they have them trained on something much more crucial: dissolving the integrity of this nation, from which no good they claim to intend will come.

George Washington himself understood this much about America, and in his famed Farewell Address gave prescient warning to "guard against the impostures of pretended patriotism." Beware of those who would seem its patriots, but who in reality seek to unravel its bonds: "There will always be reason to distrust the patriotism of those who in any quarter may endeavor to weaken its bands." For,

> within certain limits ... patriotism may look with indulgence ... upon the spirit of party. But in those of the popular character, in governments purely elective, it is a spirit not to be encouraged. ... And there being constant danger of excess, the effort ought to be by force of public opinion, to mitigate and assuage it. A fire not to be quenched, it demands a uniform vigilance to prevent its bursting into a flame, lest, instead of warming, it should consume.

Washington's warning of patriotism's *unquenchable consumption* perfectly characterizes the effect these foes of Muslims have on the American body politic. Blinded by reckless vehemence, they seek to quash the communal development and enfranchisement of the unique racial, ethnic, and cultural plurality that is America's Muslims. Yet the presence of Muslims that our voracious opponents burn to extinguish — as this community flows steadily in from the social margins — speaks with an increasingly voluble eloquence in the favor of America, both to Americans themselves and, crucially, to the world.

This contradiction grows all the more glaring. These anti-Muslim headhunters profess a desire to improve life for America's beleaguered, but they lavish their brimming budgets for "reform" — not on supporting America's harder and harder pressed — but on their crusade against American Muslim charities. Is it our humanitarian intervention on behalf of the same people whose lives they proclaim they want to better that they would prevent?

126

From Houston to Puerto Rico, from Chicago to the Navajo Nation, immoral human actions — like our fossil fuel holocaust and heart-rending racism — spawn the gales and atrocities that blow such violence through our world — ⟨corruption prevails in the land and the sea because of all the evil that the hands of humanity have earned⟩ (Sûrat Al-Rûm, 30:41) — but these afflictions clearly ⟨will not merely afflict those who do wrong among you⟩ (Sûrat Al-Anfâl, 8:25). The vulnerable pay the dearest price.

With their habitual fabrications of falsehoods against us, contemptible accusations, slanderous myths, and malicious fear-mongering — in their cruel and ignoble strive to transgress the rights of American Muslim charities and to prevent all the good we do from reaching our stricken fellows at home and the self-restrained and suppliant needy abroad — these anti-Muslim conjurers call for our very consumption.

What is this, I ask you, if not a consumption of the public good through a wanton waste of good will and a squandering of invaluable human sacrifice and material resources? Rather, my question would ring more accurately if I had stopped at the words "a consumption of the public." For these patriot charlatans, of whom Washington forewarned us, call for nothing less than a savage devouring of Muslim rights and institutions, and most directly their relief organizations.

This is not patriotism. It is societal cannibalism.

All this negativity! You may laugh when I say what comes next. My heart holds unfailing hope that today's bitter residue will yield a sweet, unforeseen fruit and untold benefit for us all tomorrow — and not because of the power of those we think mighty, but for the humility of those we hold meek.

In the Company of the Humble

America's (chronically under) reported 6.7 million Native Americans comprise this nation's most powerless people. Yet God honored us at Zakat Foundation to serve them in the earliest days of our mission. So away with the myth of American Muslim charities slighting the vulnerable to curry favor with power!

That gives you *what* we did (and do). Let me explain *why*.

We self-consciously sought to begin Zakat Foundation's relief work with the Navajo, among other disadvantaged peoples, but not for the sake of symbolism. That never informed our intent. The profound prophetic directives the Quran carries did. I mean by this the commands to morality uttered by God expressly to all the reported 124,000 emissaries He sent to human communities.* So prophethood began from the start of our creation with Adam, the first man *and* prophet, and continued down through Noah, Abraham, Moses, Jesus, and, finally, the "Seal" of prophethood, Muhammad, God's blessings of peace upon them all.

In other words, we sought only to follow upon the traces of the prophets in their eager responsiveness to their Lord's special instructions to them personally. It is this wholehearted receptivity that stitches together the spiritual fabric that produced their common godly profile, the same one we hoped to assume. The prophets are each of individual personality and character qualities but manifested in a single devoutly demeanor. I call this comportment — that is, the way the prophets walked in the world as envoys of God and yet as human beings — the prophetic stance. One divine directive that creates this posture in particular lighted our inspiration to put ourselves in the charitable service of Native Americans. I'll summarize that prophetic charge like this: *Abide among the meek and cast no longing gaze, nor lend an ear, to the people God gilds with the ornaments of this world.* But you can read this instruction to the Prophet Muhammad ﷺ for yourself:

> ❴Keep yourself patient in the company of the humble. ... Nor shall you turn your eyes from them, desiring the adornment of the life of this world. Nor shall you obey one whose heart We have rendered heedless of Our remembrance, who thus follows his whims, and whose disposition is ever disregard.❵ (Sûrat Al-Kahf, 18:28)

This prophetic imperative goes to the heart of our resolve to put Zakat Foundation in the service of America's humblest people. It came as a direct command to our Prophet ﷺ and through him to us: ❴Nor shall

---

* See the famous commentary on the Quran by Ibn Kathîr (Shaʿb ed.) 2:422-28. Also, Ibn Ḥajr in *Fatḥ al-Bârî* cites an authentic statement of the Prophet ﷺ that the number of prophets sent to humanity is 124,000 and the number of messengers is 313. Prophethood is realized when God communicates divine revelation of a Heavenly message to a human recipient chosen as a "prophet." But when God commissions a prophet to convey a new iteration of His Heavenly message to others, that prophet becomes also a messenger. Thus every messenger is a prophet, though not all prophets are messengers.

you heed the arrogant and send away the humble❯ (Sûrat Al-An‘âm, 6:52). The Quran, moreover, informs us that God required this specific conduct of all the prophets. So from the start, we have taken special care to uphold this ethic with everyone we serve in the world; for like all the heavenly commands that tailored the distinctive manner of the prophets, it comes with a required tangible behavior that substantiates it. ❮As to all of the prophets, they would, indeed, hasten to exceed one another in doing good works. … Thus they were ever humble before Us❯ (Sûrat Al-Anbiyâ', 21:90).

This description specifically weds the prophetic trait of humbleness to the physical act of rushing (not waiting till it comes to you) to do "good works," or *khayrât*, a word in the Quran that strongly implies charitable deeds. The Quran, in fact, equates (defines them in major part, actually) ❮those who humble themselves❯ with those ❮who spend in charity out of what We have provided them❯ (Sûrat Al-Ḥajj, 22:34-35). For this reason, we make a point of actively infusing this spirit of vigor in delivering charitable relief to people into our Zakat Foundation culture, no matter our recipients' location or station, condition or conviction. For the prophetic stance always sets a dynamic in motion that makes the disposition of its internal quality, in this case humbleness, visible.

We instill this (or try to) first by reminding that "humble" describes the origin of every one of us — male and female, rich and poor, whatever our language, culture, birthplace, or complexion. ❮Did We not create you human beings from a humble fluid?❯ (Sûrat Al-Mursalât, 77:20-22). We stay mindful that "humble" points at us by recalling that if we live long enough, we will be ❮reduced by old age to the most abject state of life — such that one, after having had some knowledge, will not know anything❯ (Sûrat Al-Ḥajj, 22:6). In popular parlance: *Be* the charitable deeds and disposition you'll someday need to find in others.

People think of humbleness and charity as separate things, one internal, the other external. But in reality, they both occur *inside* of us, and in tandem, a conjoined pair on a continuum that runs right through the human heart, one invariably expressing the other.

This we learn directly from the life-witness of the prophets, and it gives us our marching orders: ❮Thus strive❯ in humbleness and charity ❮for the sake of God❯. Because He has commanded it. Because He chose us for it, then made it easy for us to do it. Because that is a ❮striving that is thoroughly worthy⟩ — not of *our* personal pride, *our* individual glory, *our* natural supremacy — but ⟨of Him⟩.

So walking through this world meek and humble, rushing here and there *Niha tai hil Naha hai* — *Brings-Kindness-with-Gifts* — is neither a new way nor one of strange deportment. On the contrary, ⟨it is the sacred way of your forefather Abraham⟩ — and Abraham knew this bearing was so decisive that he honored it with a proper designation. Then he named all the people who would ever follow in his footsteps with it, wherever on earth they might be. ⟨It is he who of old has named you *Muslims* — those in willing submission to God alone⟩ (Sûrat Al-Hajj, 22:78). The Arabic title '*Muslim*' does not merely identify the followers of the religion of Islam. It names anyone whose life-struggle in benevolent sacrifice and humane service to people and creation testifies to the truth of his or her singular surrender to the Sole Divine Will. For above all other actions, God has commanded goodness.

This, the Quran tells us, is the witness the Prophet Muhammad ﷺ bore before us. Now it is our Zakat Foundation witness before all the world.

84 relief agency partners in 39 countries

ZAKAT FOUNDATION OF AMERICA

has built aid partnerships spanning the world
with outstanding humanitarian organizations

like *Mercy Corps, Jewish Voice for Peace, Feed the Children & InterAction*

8th
MYTH

MUSLIM CHARITIES SHED THEIR AMERICAN
IDENTITY AMONG MUSLIMS ABROAD

The Horse Before the Cart

*I*T'S JULY 12, 2006. I step rumpled and heavy-eyed off a 12-hour
flight from Istanbul into Chicago's Terminal 5 at O'Hare. One
step in and sobering headlines slap me awake: Bombs Blitz Lebanon by Land, Air, and Sea. I know what this means — thousands of
unsuspecting men, women, and children stampeding in panicked flight
north through a hail of bombs, missiles, and heavy artillery with nothing
but what they could snatch up and carry.

Home must wait. I rush south to Zakat Foundation's Bridgeview, Illinois,
headquarters. My colleagues have preceded me. They've already networked
for the delivery of food baskets to Lebanon's displaced. I've estimated
wrongly. A million people in vans and cars, on motorcycles and foot flood
Lebanon's roads north in a frenzy to cross the Litani and Zahrani rivers,
wishful lines of refuge. War's ceaseless skies will soon singe those hopes.
Little Lebanon's ports will hold no harbor for its civilians.

In the first hours of conflict, a lightning strike of a hundred massive
assaults detonate its Fertile Crescent into dust, including the five bridges
that span both waterways. It spares no moving vehicle. In just 34
minutes the next day — almost every 30 seconds — 59 ferocious aerial
bombardments lacerate the land from end to end. Four days in, and

Lebanon reportedly has no even remotely military targets left to destroy. Bombing persists for a month nonetheless. Everything that moves is deemed legitimate kill.

By war's end 34 days later, 11,897 sorties spewing megatons of ordinance have pummeled every possible point of significance in the tiny country. An unfathomable 170,000 artillery shells have pulverized all meaningful infrastructure. Another 2,500 missiles have scorched the earth from the sea. Explosions rocked Lebanon and shocked its unsheltered on average every 16 seconds for 34 straight days. Not the combatants, but Lebanon's innocent paid the incalculable humanitarian toll in war's only currency: blood, brick and mortar, and soul.

Impossibly, historians now report that this mammoth demolition had *meager* effect on the intended military capacity it purported to degrade as it scythed unceasingly through the length and breadth of the land. But it utterly obliterated Lebanon's civilian infrastructure: 400 miles of roads destroyed; 15,000 homes leveled; 130,000 dwellings damaged; 73 bridges wiped away; air and sea ports wrecked; water treatment and sewage plants ruined; electrical facilities devastated; 350 schools and two hospitals smashed; 900 commercial buildings flattened; 25 fuel stations incinerated.

After UN Security Council Resolution 1701 virtually ended the war on August 12, 2006, on its 31st day, fighter jets, rocket launchers, and artillery batteries spent three more days parting payloads of "submunitions." They fired 962 separate shots that sprayed an incomprehensible 4.6 million explosives, not accidentally toy-like in appearance, which blanketed dozens of southern Lebanese villages and towns. (A million unexploded munitions ensured the killing and maiming would continue into the next decade.)

In the meantime, all along the coastal road north to Beirut and routes to Syria, Lebanese Internally Displaced Persons (IDPs) waited for death or relief — under trees, in mosques, near crumbling walls and blighted structures. Packed with 58 years worth of Palestinian refugees, Lebanon had sparse infrastructure and small space for war's new wayfarers.

Into this cauldron, our aid workers waded … with spirit.

Can we use motor vehicles?

Not many left. Useless amid the rubble anyway. Almost a sure death sentence.

Our early discussions focused on how to get badly needed provisions to the suffering displaced, strewn and stranded along the pathways to Beirut, Lebanon's capital and financial center. Many of the dislocated families squatted along various arteries leading to and from the Mediterranean coastal city of Ṣaydâ, or Sidon, 27 miles to the south. The ancient Phoenician "fishing village" (mentioned prominently in the Bible, and whose name in classical Arabic (*Ṣaydûn*) means exactly that, "fishery") had grown into Lebanon's third-largest metropolitan area with about 200,000 residents.

We quickly realized that only bikes and carts could carry our food baskets to the thousands of destitute now, a daunting and manually intensive task. Our volunteers and workers jumped to it with the kind of amazing, unsung valorous feats you sometimes hear about among people in crisis. It humbles you (renews your faith in humanity), especially in the midst of such colossal manmade tragedy.

Loading. Unloading. Loading up again. They pedaled their hearts out, hour after hour, day upon day, chancing life to reach the hungry homeless. Never did they ask: *What religion? Which sect? What town?* They just served. Asked nothing in return — humanity and need the only identity and criteria of their concern.

We had a larger load of relief goods to deliver to a huddled enclave south of Ṣaydâ, the bombing still raging. A few volunteers found a horse and cart, draped an identifying Zakat Foundation of America banner on it displaying our colors and logo, packed it up, and headed out, walking.

Armed Hezbollah fighters controlled the area they entered. They stopped them. Checked the aid. The questioning began.

Zakat Foundation "of America"? You're Americans, then?

It's an American NGO. We work for them. It's distributed charitable aid to the poor and refugees here for years.

Okay, you can enter. But this name — "America" — has to go. Remove it from the banner. And these colors — red, white and blue — they have to go, too.

That's not a decision I can make.

Then you will not enter.

But we have food for the people.

Remove or return.

Our workers turned the cart around and headed back to Ṣaydâ.

One emailed me. Another called our programs department.

They're demanding we remove the name "America" from our banner and our logo colors. Or we can't get the food to the people.

I gather my directors. We talk it through. You can evaluate our thinking for yourself:

We are *Zakat Foundation of America*. We urgently want to feed these desperately needy, displaced victims of war. In fact, our donors have charged us to do just this. What we provide to the suffering as *Zakat Foundation of America* comes from our contributors — Muslims, yes, but also others — Americans all.

We represent them. They paid the charity. They instructed us to give it to all the suffering of Lebanon.

Should we block these recipients from knowing this aid comes from people in America? Will we collude in concealing this from them? What further good do we cut off if we stop these people from knowing whom this help comes from: Americans who have seen your plight. Americans whose chests hold a sense of human kinship with you. Americans who know you suffer and whose hearts have literally gone out to you. Americans who have given a charity rightfully due ❖to the indigent and the wayfarer❖ and ❖who desire only the Face of God❖ (Sûrat Al-Rûm, 30:38).

This loving-kindness, this aid, this act of human fealty and high brotherhood — this comes from *these* American people, no one else. It bears witness to the noblest principles of our Quran, our Prophet ﷺ, our religion of Islam.

To deny these recipients the right to know this — that people in America have upheld the value of the most virtuous consideration of one human being for another — violates the bedrock principles of Islam that the establishers and supporters of the Zakat Foundation *of America* built it on.

We will not remove the banner — not even a letter from the 'America' in our name and that we represent, nor a tint from the color that announces us and whom this relief comes from.

But we will proclaim to these victims the identity of the people who stopped this American Muslim humanitarian organization from feeding them today, from covering their nakedness and tending their health and wounds. This we will speak as an honest word, as the Quran commands us: ❨O you who believe! Be ever God-fearing! Thus say always a forthright word, in proper accord with God's justice and Law❩ (Sûrat Al-Aḥzâb, 33:70).

I relayed our refusal (and our promised message).

The cart of plenty — with horse properly before it — entered upon the displaced that very day. The people received their due provision, grateful with the praises of God.

❦

Of Brotherhood and Benevolence

American Muslim charities forsake their American identity among Muslims abroad. That's the myth, and the same false messaging that underlies the other propagandized fallacies anchors this one: Muslims are treacherous. They feign goodwill toward community and country, but their hearts hide hatred for America. Their religion requires this of them. It sanctions duplicity. They would seem your friend. They show you helpfulness. They hold out to you what appears an open hand but clench it against you in hostility among "their own," casting aside their camouflage and America's best interests. They lie in ambush and work to sabotage this nation. *They* are not like *us*. Never trust a Muslim.

The account I've told you of our open work as an *American* relief agency in a hostile Lebanese war zone — in fact, our insistence on blazoning our national identity, *even at gunpoint* — could not more dramatically refute the misconception of American Muslim infidelity and cloaked intent.

But do not think this a light decision. It was morally fraught.

We had cause to comply with the demand to remove the name and colors of America from our banner. Hungry, sick, exposed, dispossessed people urgently awaited the sustenance we carried. The lives of our workers stood at risk. We put Zakat Foundation's broader humanitarian mission itself in Lebanon on the line. Others (with hearts as sound as we hope ours to be) may well see our decision as ethically misguided or at least precarious.

So what principles girded our judgment, or did we just fly by the seat of our pants?

In the vignette that opens this chapter, I hinted at one of the principles that guided our decision-making that day. I said that people in America had upheld the value of *the most virtuous consideration of one human being for another*. This statement alludes to a mutual duty of charitable compassion and human connection that the Quran reminds us God has bound all people by, regardless of faith or affiliation.

> ﴾O humankind! Be ever God-fearing, conscious of your Lord who created all of you from a single soul — and from it created its mate, and from them both spread abroad many men and women. So fear God, in whose name you ask consideration of one another. And,

138

therefore, be dutiful to kindred. For, indeed, ever is God vigilant over all of you.❯ (Sûrat Al-Nisâ', 4:1)

This verse tells us that God created all of us from a common father and mother. *You know them.* Adam and Eve. He recalls to us our shared parentage to reawaken in us that most defining of all human instincts, compassion, the reflex to care for one another, which may have gone dormant beneath the suffocating material thrall of the life of this world. This Heavenly reminder of our mutual humanity, moreover, has come down for a reason: to elicit from us a response of *tenderness expressed*, originally native in us — especially for those whom life and circumstance have made weak before us; especially for those our eyes see brought in humility to their knees.

The purpose of this divine recall notice on our humanity, then — when we behold the suffering of our siblings in the world — is to jolt us into an elemental recollection of our own humanity, such that our human benevolence will speak with a clear voice inside us and our sensory hearts will hear it, as if saying to us: *Here sigh my cherished brothers and sisters. Here cry our precious children. Calamity has struck them. Wretchedness covers them. They are of me. They could be me.*

That's the call of the wakened human soul. Then the heart's summons to action goes out.

Come sweet kindness!

And for our fellows in distress:

They are hungry: Eat of my food. *They are naked:* Take from my cloth. *They are crying:* Be soothed in my solace. *They are injured:* I dress your wounds. *They are homeless:* Shade in my shelter.

I have not explained the implication and aspiration of this verse on the fly. Someone angelically taught illustrated its human purpose and power for us:

> We were with the Prophet ﷺ [in his Mosque] on the cusp of dawn when a people barely covered with sleeveless sheets or clad in woolen rags came to him. … The face of the Prophet ﷺ changed when he saw they suffered deprivation. He entered his home and came out, instructed Bilal [his caller to prayer], who summoned the people to prayer then called them to stand for it. The Prophet ﷺ led prayer then addressed us. He said:

139

❴O humankind! Be ever God-fearing, conscious of your Lord who created all of you from a single soul — and from it created its mate, and from them both spread abroad many men and women. So fear God, in whose name you ask consideration of one another. And, therefore, be dutiful to kindred. For, indeed, ever is God vigilant over all of you.❵ (Sûrat Al-Nisâ', 4:1)

He also recited the verse … : ❴O you who believe! Be ever God-fearing! And let every soul look to what it has forwarded for tomorrow❵ (Sûrat Al-Ḥashr, 59:18). A man gave in charity of his gold, another of his coin, another of his robe, another of his measure-full of wheat, another of his measure-full of dates — whereupon the Prophet ﷺ said: '[Give] if only half a date.'

Then a man of the Ansar [the Muslims of Madinah] came with a sack so full his hands could barely hold it. Rather, they couldn't even hold it!

Then the people came forward [with their charity] one after the other, until I saw two heaps of food and clothes. That's when I saw the face of the Prophet ﷺ shining bright as the moon, as if glittering gold, and he said:

'One who sets a precedent in Islam of good doing, for him is its reward and the reward of all who act on it after him, diminishing nothing of their reward. And one who sets a precedent in Islam of evildoing, upon him is its burden and the burden of all who act on it after him, diminishing nothing of their burdens.'" (*Muslim*, 1 no. 171)

The Prophet ﷺ no more than recited the verse *of asking consideration of one another* — reminding people of the one father and mother of us all, our unbreakable human bonds, our irrevocable responsibility for each other's welfare, and reminded that we will meet our deeds again before God hereafter — than their hearts beat suddenly anew with that instinctual feeling of common humanity, and they began to give without stint. You can imagine also how this wakened an abiding reciprocal sensation of human fraternity and fellowship in the chests of these penniless poor.

That's exactly the sense of kinship in our linked humanity we in the Zakat Foundation wanted to kindle between our afflicted Lebanese recipients and our American donors, for true relief — as its 'humanitarian' name implies — entails more than nourishing the body. It should reaffirm the "humanity" of the anguished and imprint in their psyches

140

the profound concern and inherent affection their fellow human beings hold for them.

It's easy enough to claim feelings of compelling nationalism, an unrivaled patriotism, as our Zakat Foundation motivation for keeping America's name and colors on our banner — easy *and* cheap. Virtue, however, for all of us lies in our self-restrained remembrance of our common clay origin, the upright balance of our human stature, the simple humanity of us all. This is humility, the most elevating of all human dispositions. Indeed, both names — 'human' and 'humility' — share an ultimate linguistic origin: 'of the earth' — which also points to the *source* for the name of our one father, Adam, the meaning of which relates to the 'earth's surface,' his 'earthen color,' and his creation from 'mud' — that is, the dust of the earth, the ultimate ancestry and earthly end of us all.

Of Hope and Friendship

By our stand on that day — to burnish our humanitarian organization's Americanness and broadcast the American identity of those who gave *of their wealth and their measures* — we tried to tether both need *and* compassion to the truth. We sought to lift the eyes of people past the baseless pride of bordered thinking to an acknowledgment of one another grounded in twin realities: our humanity links us to every other person, and our deeds define the level of our humanity.

Tell me, then, the meaningful difference between the position of the Hezbollah fighters blocking our distribution of charitable aid to innocent victims of war, ostensibly because of the nation we and our aid come from (and many of us are Muslims!) and the stance of those in America whose profession it has become to fight Muslims, who seek to obstruct Muslim charities from gathering and delivering aid to the poor and the stricken at home and abroad, supposedly for the sake of the nation we live in (and we are Americans!).

What nonsense! What sham ideological drivel! And to what end, to bluster about the purity of our own persons? Well, you and I, we're just children of Adam, and Adam is from dust.

My colleagues and I harbor no desire to deny or delete differences between people. From one, and then two — ❨O humankind! Indeed, We have created all of you from a single male and female❩ — has spread many. We see this as a sign of God's power and a wellspring of rectitude and increase for us. But we need to see our multiplicity through the eyes God has intended — ❨We have made you peoples and tribes, so that you may come to know one another❩ — not to hate each other, but to recognize and admire groups and nations for the gifts and outlooks God has developed in them.

This was not just about maintaining the integrity of our name. We wanted the Lebanese recipients of this aid to know who it came from in order to strengthen the bond of human togetherness and harmony, to reemphasize what would have been lost if "America" was taken out of the name. This aid that came specifically for the people in Lebanon would have lost its meaning, its significance — it would signify far less — if we did not disclose who specifically thought about them and sent it. It would no longer have been a communication from one particular people to another. It would no longer have been a disclosure of subjects, of "the who" that human beings crave and need to know, which is the bedrock of countering violence.

Our external expressions of profusion and culture display in us a standing miracle but evidence no special honor, requiring of us neither striving in good works nor modesty's beautifying self-restraint. When we attempt to locate our distinction in these outer aspects of our humanity, we deviate from the pathways of peace to the perversions of pride. Our descent into misguidance and cruelty becomes inevitable.

The human being's honor inheres in his or her humility, ❨for, indeed, the noblest of you in the sight of God is the most God-fearing of you❩. It is all about how faithfully we act on our natural human longing to free our higher humanity, which occurs in exact proportion to how well we subdue our lowly (and equally native) capacity for brutality. If we fall to the latter of these inclinations, we will not escape its cascade of horrific consequences. ❨Indeed, God is all-knowing, all-aware❩ (Sûrat Al-Ḥujarât, 49:13).

So know this: *we* choose and *we* act, ❨and not equal are the good deed and the evil deed❩. We learned this from the Prophet ﷺ in the account of the destitute who came to him. Each of us has the chance to initiate the charity of a benevolent act, and then reap its goodness and the good of everyone who benefits and follows suit, or to bar it and harvest its harm, and the harmfulness of all who do the same.

Then as to those who set themselves against our charity and humanitarian work — whether foreign or domestic — our position of humility in Zakat Foundation stays the same: ❮Repel their evildoing with that which is best in the sight of God❯; for our faith teaches us to believe in the transformative power of doing good. ❮Then, behold! The one who had enmity for you, and for whom you had enmity, may become like a most intimate friend.❯ This promise set a hopeful keystone in our resolve to give aid to Lebanon's war-ravaged in the face of combatants — the *America* in our name and its colors flying free in the full light of day. It lays a cornerstone, as well, in the promise of friendship with contenders at home.

It breathes hope in us still. For we know ❮none shall attain this but those who are patient in suffering. And none shall attain this but one endowed with a magnificent share of goodness❯ (Sûrat Fuṣṣilat, 41:34-35).

14,756

The number of girls and women on four continents that
— in 2017 alone —
ZAKAT FOUNDATION OF AMERICA
empowered with safe shelter, skills and business training

9th
MYTH

American Muslim Charities
Underrepresent Muslim Women

Indeed, the Muslim men and the Muslim women,
and the believing men and the believing women,
and the devoutly obedient men and the devoutly obedient women,
and the truthful men and the truthful women,
and the patient men and the patient women,
and the reverent men and the reverent women,
and the charitable men and the charitable women,
and the fasting men and the fasting women,
and the men who guard their chastity
    and the women who guard theirs,
and the men who remember God much
    and the women who remember Him —
for these, God has prepared forgiveness and a magnificent reward.
– The Quran (Sûrat Al-Aḥzâb, 33:35)

Figs and Other Fruits

*T*HE SMALL BOY stood, half hidden amid the rows of fruit trees. The long, slender fig trunks of his family grove went up and up. Their branches seemed to pierce the clouds.

No. Not under some foreign vault of blue, but there, under the Turkish sky.

He watched the birds. He loved them. But they loved the figs, poking holes in their meaty fruits with their beaks. Pocked figs didn't bring

145

much at market. So his mother would send him to fend off the birds in the days before harvest time. He took to his task eagerly, a pocketful of stones and an impressive repertoire of clamor, both for throwing to scare off the alighting flocks. Pressed but happy, their orchards gave them a little windfall of autumn money.

A village path ran near the fig trees through their land.

"My dear son," the mother would tell him, without fail. "Only two kinds of people pass this way: people from the far hamlets who've walked a long time, headed home or away; and the very poor.

"Figs freshen the traveler and feed the poor. So if any pass, be sure to offer them figs and don't skimp. The figs you give them do not lessen our figs. It increases them. For everyone who passes through our land is our guest, and every guest carries with him a blessing. If you give, our figs grow. If you offer, you gain. So don't be shy."

So each time someone passed by, the boy would run to him, figs in hand. "My uncle! My uncle!" He would call out. "I have figs for you. Please eat them."

The travelers would laugh. The hungry would smile. They would take the figs, eat them, and call down blessings, on the boy and his family, from the One they love above.

No. Not under some foreign vault of blue, but there, under the Kurdish sky, where the fig trees — and I — grew.

Giving, the Secret of Blessing

My life story begins there, beneath fig and fruit tree, under a stretch of Kurdish sky, and the lowered wing of a mother who loved giving for the Face of God so dearly she watered the depths of her son's heart with it.

These boyhood lessons of outlook, of giving, of running breathless to the struggling and needy guests God sends you, have stayed with me this past half-century and more. I didn't know then she intended to inculcate me with the literal teachings and way of the Prophet ﷺ, who said: "Charity does not diminish the wealth of its giver. Nor does God increase His servant who pardons others in anything but honor. And none humbles himself for the sake of God save God elevates him" (*Muslim*).

My mother sought to make sure I grew into a giver; that I knew if I shared, it would never shrink what I have. Rather, it would bring blessings and growth to my wealth. I am grateful every day for having such a mother. For whatever good character that boy may have come to today, he definitely has his mother to thank for it.

Yet I have since realized that many a Muslim woman follows upon this prophetic pattern of generosity, selflessness, and striving. They contribute charitably. They manage the giving groves of the world. They raise children to conscious benevolence toward others. They organize aid committees in their community mosques and centers. They preside over nonprofits that care for the abused, heal the sick and wounded, and protect the vulnerable. They lead critical agencies within international humanitarian institutions. They direct national programs and regional offices for American Muslim charities in Asia, Africa, the Middle East, and Latin America.

Not lightly do I specify this charitable work of Muslim women, nor the critical responsibilities they have assumed in our global relief organizations. Every one of these spheres of humanitarian action at Zakat Foundation has a woman guiding it or directly carrying out its work. That's not happenstance. Women comprise half our directors. They make up at least 50 percent of our program administrators and department coordinators and some 60 percent of Zakat Foundation's cadre of aid workers.

I'll make no attempt to take credit for this heavy representation of women in the middle and upper management of our American Muslim charity and throughout our organization. That recognition, I'll again accord to my mother.

Yet historically Muslim women have always functioned in the lead of these kinds of complex finance-centered endeavors. When the souk of Madinah, the main market in the City of the Prophet ﷺ, grew vast and its business relationships intricate, and the celebrated second Caliph ʿUmar ibn Al-Khaṭṭâb determined it needed someone to set regulations for it in the public benefit and to adjudicate problems between buyers and sellers, he appointed Al-Shifâ' bint ʿAbdullah to that position, a woman, and one of the earliest followers of the Prophet ﷺ. (Her given name seems to have been Layla. She became known by the title Al-Shifâ' as a widely respected physician. She also taught reading and writing.) When the Makkan market reached the same or greater proportions, he designated a controller for it, as well — another woman, Samrâ' bint Nuhayk.

Women, then, have always taken a place in the vanguard of this kind of work. I could no more found and direct an international Muslim humanitarian organization without women in its leadership — not simply to represent their gender but owing to their qualified, capable and deserving leadership in their own right — than I could have neglected to give figs of refreshment to the passersby along the road through our fruited woodlands at the instruction of my mother.

And was she not a Muslim woman, like her forebears, Al-Shifâ' and Samrâ', and countless others unnamed? *In their hijab. In their covering garments.*

Were they not the foundations of their households and communities; the instillers of prophetic character in their families and societies; the first schools for their children and their civilization?

How, then, will you call the Muslim woman oppressed?

False Presumptions and the First Muslim Woman

Years later, I left the figs and vines of our little farm for Switzerland and its universities. I recall a professor of sociology beginning one of my courses with an earnest lecture on the categorical oppression of Muslim women — followed in every subsequent class with that same oration, as though it were the foundation of all truth about society. After weeks, I decided to engage her on the basis of my own experience.

"The Muslim woman you keep telling us about, why have I not seen

148

her in my culture? I come from a little Muslim village, in a Muslim district, in a Muslim society. Yet as I listen to you, I find that this woman you describe doesn't exist.

"You have not characterized my mother, my aunts, or my sisters. On the contrary, the women I have seen, as I educate myself, strike me now as visionaries and incomparably thoughtful. I grant they do not all have university degrees. Yet they live as repositories of wisdom and learning. They raise well-adjusted, polite children — a diminishing but vital social skill that seems to me worthy of serious study. They manage households and supporting businesses with efficiency and success. They create and govern the social organizations of their communities.

"Also, I see several of the largest Muslim countries in the world all having had women presidents or prime ministers. Politics aside, by the measure of human leadership a number of Muslim societies seem poised to follow [a correct forecast, as that number has now risen to 10].

"In addition, your conclusions do not make sociological sense, I mean, that *every* Muslim society oppresses *all* women, to the extent that these pathetic human beings play no serious role in social life at all.

"Finally, let me add that history reports that the believing women around the Prophet Muhammad ﷺ, and for fourteen hundred years since, have contributed crucially to the establishment of his message and the extraordinary growth of the Muslim community. Women, in fact, constituted the heavy majority of most of his followers in Makkah. Also, the guiding Text of the Muslims, the Quran, holds up Mary ﷺ, the mother of Jesus ﷺ, as a specifically exemplary model — not merely for women, but for all believing human beings, along with Âsiyah, the wife of Pharoah, another remarkable paradigm of faith. Both these women the Quran shows as exceedingly present, active, and capable at the highest and most profound echelons of society and in their communities most crucial times. Again, the Quran presents them as role models for all the believing, men and women alike.

> ¢God sets forth, as an example for those who believe, the wife of Pharoah. Behold, she said: My Lord! Build for me near You a house in the Garden of Paradise. And deliver me from Pharoah and his evildoing. And deliver me from the wrongdoing people. Moreover, there is Mary, daughter of ʿImrân, who safeguarded her chastity.

Then We breathed into her womb of Our life-giving spirit. For she confirmed the revealed words of her Lord and His Heavenly Books. Indeed, she was ever of those who are devoutly obedient.❭ (Sûrat Al-Taḥrîm, 66:11-12)

"I could go on. But let me say plainly, I think you don't have a clue about Muslim women and the sources of their oppression today, of which your teaching constitutes one."

This may seem harsh, but I cannot say strongly enough how the idea that Muslim women as a category stand as the exemplars of oppression in our times struck me as completely foreign and unrelatable, having no resonance in my heart or familiarity to my mind.

Yet this professor's articulated view on Muslim women as the archetypally oppressed remains a mainstream view in modern culture. For those of us who claim a conscientious and literate awareness as Muslims — and I remind that I grew up in a humble village of southeastern Turkey — our experience of Muslim women roots us in a reality that notably diverges from this image.

Muslims — both men and women — have addressed the lives of women and the practical and religious issues of gender for more than a thousand years. They have filled libraries with its multilayered discourse in many languages. I'll provide here three examples, familiar to most Muslims, which illustrate our real outlook on women.

The first comes from the Quran. It speaks to the Muslim's spiritual perspective.

The second we take from the Prophet ﷺ. Known as the *Sunnah*, what he did, said, and approved, which guides the application of Islam in life. It clarifies the practical historical foundation that emerged in the implementation of Heavenly Revelation.

The third shows the intellectual and cultural expression of Muslims in our civilization and gives a sense of the Muslim social milieu. My aim is to give concrete meaning to the esteem of the Muslim woman in the eyes of Muslims who understand and care about living by the religious and moral underpinnings of Islam.

Women in Revelation

You've already seen two significant statements of the Divine on women from the verses of Revelation in the Quran. The first crowns this

150

chapter. It inventories the ten jeweled qualities of those God will forgive on the Day of Judgment, and by His grace reward in the Hereafter with everlasting admission into the Gardens of Paradise. Take a moment to re-read it, if you would, for none of the other Heavenly Books (and as a matter of faith Muslims believe in them all) contains any passage like it.

It tells us unmistakably that God in Islam accords no special spiritual superiority to men over women. Nor does He diminish the standard of His equal expectations for either male or female believer — neither in how He requires them to act on their professed belief, nor in the principled standards His religion prescribes for them to uphold so that they may sustain their own moral integrity and maintain society's.

In other words, the Muslim disposition set by the Quran judges humanity, not by gender, but by one's proclaimed belief *along with* the actions one does that either bear out or belie that belief. Gendered competition and the illusive frames of mind and reference to which it leads do *not* issue from the worldview of Islam. Nor does this constitute the native Muslim perspective or the civilization it built and seeks to express.

The second verse of the Quran you've read here is the one that hails Mary 🌸, Mother of Jesus 🌸 and Âsiyah, wife of Pharaoh, as exemplary. What I stated previously about them suffices.

The new (and first of three examples of women) I wish now to present occurs in the Quran. Every aware Muslim knows that the women around the Messenger 🌸 made up a vocal segment of society. They had strong voices, readily deployed. Indeed, some of their dialogues with the Prophet 🌸, and supplications, God Himself captures and incorporates in the Quran. This means Muslims may recite them in their obligatory Five Daily Ritual Prayers. Any recitation of the complete Word of God necessarily must include the voices of these women. In effect, they comprise part of our liturgy.

Here, for example, you may read the Divine Revelation — part of the Quran — that came down in response to a woman named Khawlah bint Tha'labah, complaining of a means effecting divorce that Arabs used before Islam to repudiate their wives.

⟨Truly, God has heard the words of she who has argued before you, O Prophet, concerning her husband, she who has made complaint to God. ... Those of you who sinfully estrange themselves from their wives with a mere pronouncement ... they are assuredly utter-ing an abominable statement and falsehood.❯ (Surat Al-Mujâdilah, 58:1-2)

This shows that from their earliest history Muslim women did not hesitate to enter into discourse, even with the Prophet Muhammad ﷺ, on the most serious matters and in a forceful way. God Himself, in fact, characterizes Khawlah's interaction with His Prophet ﷺ as her having "argued" her case with him, and in this she persisted in search of change and the vindication of her rights and that of all women. She did not hold back, nor did Muslim women withhold their judgments and positions, even in the realm of objections and discussions with the Prophet Mu-hammad ﷺ.

That female Muslim voice has consistently continued articulating itself to authority and in decisive social arguments even after the time of the Prophet ﷺ. In fact, we meet Khawlah again when ʿUmar, the most robust and resolute of men, assumed the reigns of leadership over a vast expanse of peoples and territory as Caliph. Now aged, she saw him in the street and halted him, as the renowned 14th-century Syrian scholar Ibn Kathîr reports her words:

"ʿUmar! Remember you were once called Little ʿUmar [as a boy]. Then you were called ʿUmar [in full]. Now you are called Commander of the Faithful [as leader and commander-in-chief of the Muslim community]. Fear God, O ʿUmar! For very truly, one certain of death fears loss, and one most convinced of the coming Judgment fears punishment."

ʿUmar stood silent, listening to her. She parted, and his compan-ions asked: "Why did you permit this old woman to detain you in this [unbecoming] manner?"

"I swear by God," said ʿUmar, "had she held me from dawn till day's end, I would not have parted from her, except to pray the obligatory prayers. Do you not know who this woman is? She is Khawlah bint Thaʿlabah. ❮Truly, God has heard❯ her words from above the Seven Heavens. Will God heed her words and ʿUmar will not?"

Since the days of the Prophet ﷺ and divine revelation, then, Muslim women have spoken out freely and received reverent ear. Any informed

Muslim well knows this. The argument and prayers of Muslim women remain enshrined as an indelible part of Muslim cultures and the principle source of this faith.

Women in the Life of the Prophet ﷺ

In this light, I introduce you to undoubtedly the foremost woman in the mind of all Muslims, Khadijah, the wife of the Prophet ﷺ. Take in her description from the first books of prophetic biography (whose writings begin with the youngest Companions of the Prophet ﷺ himself):

> Khadijah was a merchant woman of prestige and wealth ... a woman of consequence, capable and steadfast, and of high nobility. ... Indeed, in her time, she was in lineage the central woman of the [noblest Arab tribe of] Quraysh, the greatest of women in prestige and the most plentiful of women in wealth. Every man of her people was eager to marry her, if they could but attain to it. (*Al-Mukhtaṣir*, 1:130-31)

At the time of her marriage to the Prophet ﷺ, Khadijah was 40, a mature woman altogether experienced in life and entirely fathoming of it. Her people esteemed her with the title "Lady of the Women of Quraysh." Yet, she was more than the sum of her pedigree and wealth. With the epithet *Al-Ṭâhirah*, "The Woman of Purity," they hailed, as well, her impeccable virtue, for she was devoutly righteous and endowed with an expansive intellect. Twice married before wedding herself to the Prophet ﷺ, the Prophet ﷺ by contrast was poor, orphaned at birth (by the death of his father, with the loss of his mother at 6), and about the age of Khadijah's children at the time of their marriage — all conditions that could not recommend him in the life of a noble woman, particularly to one of "Lady" Khadijah's station.

Writes a contemporary female Muslim scholar, a Syrian refugee, incidentally (in the translated words of my colleague):

> Without exception, Khadijah was her era's most illustrious woman. ... Hers were the first ears to hear Revelation from the Messenger of God ﷺ. To her the Prophet ﷺ was commanded to convey the particular greetings of God borne by the Arch-Angel Gabriel ﷺ — and how momentous an event it was, especially in the world of the oppressed women of that time! It is as if God — the Creator of time

153

and place, Beholder of every age — meant to make humanity realize the high station and worth of *woman*, and to epitomize her natural and necessary participation in all the ways of calling people to God; to establish for humanity that, in truth, *woman* is a competent agent of *ʿaqîdah*, that is, of relaying the call of God's "creed of Oneness," and well able to partake in lofting the standard of the summons to God.

This same refugee scholar makes a most interesting point about Khadijah, one quite relevant to the current notion of the oppressed Muslim female, which in so many ways proceeds from the misunderstanding of the quality that most defines the essence of the Muslim character and community; namely, modesty — a consideration that cannot fail to inspirit the Muslim woman's outlook on her public presentation, demeanor, and dress.

If one comes from a culture no longer familiar with the impulse to cover one's physical adornments, or that has ceased valorizing bodily modesty and chasteness, or that does not heed monotheistic religion's or tradition's call for publicly concealing the sensual aspects of our appearance, or that sees only inequality and no wisdom in articulating a boundary etiquette in the intermingling of men and women, then one should not assume these expressions of reserve in the Muslim woman indicate her oppression, or naiveté, or backwardness, or prudishness, or uneducated ignorance. Rather, life has paths, and the Muslim woman may simply follow upon another that she believes will ease her in her journey to the places she wants to go — a journey she has dressed for.

The Muslim Woman as Vitally Esteemed Teacher

I spoke of my mother earlier, not as a son extolling the womb that bore him (though that's a good ethic for us all), but harking back to a deep tradition among Muslims: Women have always comprised an integral part of our learned community. The Muslim woman scholar stands as an absolute fixture in our history, with no question about her comparable quality to male counterparts.

From Islam's inception, Muslim women have exerted an unabated and determinative impact in virtually all fields, from medicine to martial arts, from business to farming. They have formed a pillar of every educative field, secular and sacred. But one in particular is crucial and essentially formative for all Muslims who would live their faith: The religious

154

science of *hadîth*, the conveyed statements, approvals, and practices of the Prophet ﷺ regarding implementing the will of God in life. For Muslims, *hadîth* reports constitute an augmenting stream of divine revelation, along with the Quran, which they indispensably delineate. You cannot live the latter without the former.

This possibility, of adhering to the specified guidance of the Prophet ﷺ, only remains because of the meticulous dedication and compilation of these *hadîth* reports — linked by verified transmitters and through authenticated texts of transmission — back to what the Prophet ﷺ actually did, said, or approved of.

Without the women scholars of *hadîth* from the time of the Prophet ﷺ through every generation until our own, these reports would never have survived. Writes history of *hadîth* authority Muhammad Zubayr Siddiqi in his *Women Scholars of Ḥadîth*:

> History records few scholarly enterprises, at least before modern times, in which women have played an important and active role side by side with men. The science of *hadîth* forms an outstanding exception in this respect. Islam, a religion, which (unlike Christianity) refused to attribute gender to the Godhead, and never appointed a male priestly elite to serve as an intermediary between creature and Creator, started life with the assurance that while men and women are equipped by nature for complementary rather than identical roles, no spiritual superiority inheres in the masculine principle.

Hungarian scholar Ignaz Goldziher, one of the founders of modern Islamic studies in Europe, had this to say about the foremost *hadîth* compilation of Islam, the *Ṣaḥîḥ* of *Al-Bukhârî*:

> Women occupy an eminent place in the history of the transmission of the text of *Ṣaḥîḥ Al-Bukhârî*. The most famous source of the text is a woman called Karîmah bint Aḥmad from Marw (d. 462 in Mecca). No transmitter of *Bukhârî* could compete with her *isnâd* [chains of *hadîth* report transmissions].

Karîmah appears as but one female source in *hadîth* scholarship. A look at the complete chains of *hadîth* transmissions in these compilations shows the constant presence of women in relating this part of revelation. No Muslim second-guesses these women or judges their scholarship on a scale different than a man's.

We vaunt women today for reaching stations of prestige in corporations, medicine, politics, literature, even the media, because we see them as having broken through the red tape and shattered glass ceilings in defeating immeasurable odds to gain essentially a monetary value equal to that of a male counterpart. And undoubtedly many cultures have placed women in the position of having to defend and demand their unalienable rights.

I now understand my Swiss sociology professor's outlook on Muslim women, within the assumptions of her larger worldview, in this light. In the culture in which she had emerged and studied, the plight and fight of women reads as nothing less than harrowing. Some two decades after Khadijah (the wife of the Prophet ﷺ to whom I introduced you just before) had received the Heavenly salutations of God Himself through the Arch-Angel Gabriel ﷺ — the import of which lies deeply imbedded in the consciousness of every Muslim woman as to her own invaluable worth and possibility — a quite different "welcome" to women played out among the bishops of the Council of Macon, in Burgundy, France (585 CE).

They had gathered there to study, for creedal purposes, the "affair of woman": *Does she have a soul? Is it a soul eligible for redemption in the Hereafter or not?* The Council of Lyon did at last decree that woman was indeed possessed of a human soul — but an irredeemable one, nonetheless, one that could not be delivered in the Hereafter to Paradise, save for that of Mary ﷺ, mother of Jesus ﷺ.

Against this backdrop of such patriarchal ignorance, the women of the Euro-American tradition fought back with their hands and minds, with their hearts, and yes, even with their souls.

This "affair of woman" has never ceased to be objectified and used for the material gain of a patriarchal elite. In our times — the era of free-for-all myth-making and maligning of Muslims — Muslim women continue to suffer from the fallacies "European writers have been circulating about them from the 17th century onwards," writes Ahmad Gunny, Fellow at the Oxford Center for Islamic Studies, an expert in French, Voltaire, and 18th-century European literature, in his *Perceptions of Islam in European Writings*. Those of us living in the diaspora of European cultures, and, indeed, throughout global society, too often acquiesce in these old, false notions of the much-misunderstood Muslim woman. In the past, these misconceptions "subsequently developed into European chauvinism at the expense of Muslim women."

A similarly dangerous pattern of jingoism has once more emerged in the world. "Today, there is one constant," writes University of Michigan Professor Juan Cole. In America, "Muslims [have been made] our enemy of the first order," and this "Islamophobia is reinforced by an ugly resurgence of fascism in Germany, Italy, Hungary, and other European countries."

This resurgent chauvinism has likewise spawned flawed ideas of the oppressed Muslim woman that have proven just as virulent in our times. You have heard these menacing cultural assumptions ring out as the literal battle cries of countless devastating wars of invasion of predominantly Muslim societies, setting off a cascade of unprecedented humanitarian catastrophes in our own 21st century. *Save the burka'd woman. Rescue the female from the veil. Free the girl to go to school.* Here's America's former Secretary of Defense James Mattis:

> You go into Afghanistan, you got guys who slap women around for five years because they didn't wear a veil. You know, guys like that ain't got no manhood left anyway. So it's a hell of a lot of fun to shoot them. Actually, it's quite fun to fight them, you know. It's a hell of a hoot. It's fun to shoot some people. I'll be right up there with you. I like brawling.

Nearly 18 years, $1.07 trillion, and up to a million dead later — including burka-wearing mothers, veiled sisters, and little school girls — you begin to see the dreadful human cost of this terrible, paternalistic, culturally arrogant assumption about Muslim women and oppression. Indeed, I see it every day, as do my humanitarian organizational peers, in a world of vilified refugees, widows, and orphans; of young amputees and permanently traumatized children; and the starving and disease-suffering in proportions never before seen on this earth.

What fig leaf, from what grove, will cover over humanity's shame from the calamitous consequence of this misconception?

THE INDISPENSABLE PLACE

OF THE AMERICAN MUSLIM CHARITY

I BEGAN THIS BOOK with a Turkish parable to answer a question: *What is the Zakat Foundation?* It's the simple story of two earnest men, a thriving bread maker and a workman in dire need. The baker wants to show God his gratitude for His blessings with the best his hands can put forth, the perfect bread loaf, and entreats Him sincerely to accept it. The laborer, penniless and hungry, beseeches God to nourish him with the provision he needs to go on striving in search of God's bounty, so he may gratefully sustain his family. The men never see each other. Only their prayers meet ... in the mosque, the open expanses of the House of God. There, gift is given and provender received, the supplication of each satisfied.

Zakat Foundation, I explained, is the convergence of these two prayers.

The subtler lesson of this parable, I did not state directly in my telling of it but spent the rest of this book's ink spelling it out. I'll say it plainly now. Think about the special place in the world that the mosque in this tale represents. It is the open, societal setting that propels the prayers of these men to life. It is that unmonitored physical, communal exchange that proves indispensable in catalyzing their pleas to Heaven, then ushering them to material fulfillment here on earth. It is in essence *the sacrosanct space of freedom that every society needs* to make possible the most elementally human of all transactions: charity, the human right of giver to give and receiver to receive, freely.

This is not done for the sake of accruing to oneself power, or possession, or self-interest. It is not done to socially stroke one's personal vanity or to preen oneself in public. Its far deep intention is rather more humanly beautiful, a vitally humanizing impulse. Its Quranic expression I have already taught you: *Seeking only the Face of God.* That is the urgent instinct coursing free in our veins, a present will to soothe our fellow human beings and be soothed by them. Acting on this inclination is, in fact, tantamount to the God-given right to be fully human. I mean by this to say, we human beings have a divine mandate to freely be the clay creatures we so plainly are: inspirited by Heaven with a soul of compassion, a heart of kindness, a mind of empathy and consideration, and, yes, a body and being of great need and greater vulnerability.

The loss of all this we suffer — in our essential humanity — when our timidity bests us, and we allow ourselves to be bullied into letting this preeminently inviolate charitable space in society contract; and this we have done. The stakes could not be higher, and all of us stand in stricken witness of the catastrophe this decline of man's free sacred spaces is unleashing in the world.

We live in times that trust in, even hallow, a free market and unbound currencies. Its advocates condemn as heretical business regulation, as nihilistic monetary control. Yet they view with suspicion, disdain, any lingering aperture in human society that permits the unimpeded flow of aid, in kind or cash, to help the suffering. Those who warn of brimstone, should this fiscal fundamentalism be breached, have now grown so bold as to belie the naiveté of material altruism and to decry charity as nothing more than a chink in an increasingly mailed financial world order.

It so happens that these high priests of finance also control most of the world's political and banking machinery. Hence, the inalienable field of free humane action and humanitarian right is exactly the margin that world governments, regulative authorities, and our suddenly free-market-immune, too-big-to-fail bank bishops have been systematically squeezing to the point of sucking the oxygen out of the open air that people and their charities require to carry out their societal obligations

160

and missions of uplifting the poor, saving the afflicted, and reestablishing the uprooted.

This throttling of the financial flow of relief agencies twists in a telling helix. It runs in parallel with the ruinous rise of an ever-smaller, connected clique of impossibly moneyed elites. Their freedoms to enrich themselves lawlessly, unaccountably, and with neither institutional nor public moral oversight are expanding exponentially and (this is telling) in exact proportion to the diminishment of global, public wealth and the fading freedom of people to give of their means to whomever they choose that suffers without.

There is still another wrinkle. Research after study now demonstrates beyond doubt that while Muslim charities are the most crucial links in a calamitously overstretched and fragmenting global humanitarian chain stretching across the humanly devastated middle of the earth (where the vast majority of Muslims live), the presence of the interlinked Muslim charity is also the scarcest. Little wonder, for though Muslim international relief organizations consistently demonstrate the highest levels of public, fiscal transparency and strict implementation of established humanitarian financial ethics, they nonetheless remain far and away the most unfairly targeted institutions by the world's governmental oversight agencies and monetary stewards.

There's more. The planet's biggest banks — compulsory conduits (or gatekeepers) in the international humanitarian cycle — increasingly cry fear of governmental inquiry into dauntless Muslim charities that provide relatively minuscule global relief to Muslim peoples utterly ravaged by war, displacement, starvation, disease, and poverty. This makes such banks "regrettably but necessarily" risk averse to maintaining these Muslim charities' accounts, without which they simply cannot function. Yet the stunning Panama Papers' whistle-blowing leaks and subsequent worldwide journalistic investigations tell us quite another tale, one of intrepid, swashbuckling bankers flouting both government and regulatory bureaus. These same behemoth-bank executives too chilled to chance the accounts of audited Muslim charities that are perhaps in a low-level Treasury Department official's purview have shown no similar qualms in wagering everything in their diligent, harrowing, relentless pursuit to abet politicians, dictators, kings, the uber-rich, corporate executives (including their own), celebrities, and out-and-out criminals in laundering and hiding their taxless, secreted, and ill-gotten gains of billions of dollars in endless chains of offshore shell organizations managed by pauper, puppet directors.

I am not railing here without purpose and prescription. There is a method to this global madness of skyrocketing wealth for an ever-shrinking glitterati of hundreds while the unwashed millions tailspin into beggary. Underpinning this contradiction and the diminishing sacred space for goodly human transaction lies the well-funded, myth-making, media machinery that generates and promulgates the egregious stereotypes that vilify Muslims and disinform the public about Islam.

That seems a pixelated picture, but let us connect the dots.

These trends of shrinking transactional public free space, diminishing mass global wealth, unprecedented explosion of human suffering, mega-aggregation of uncountable riches in the hands of fewer and fewer individuals, aggression against and suppression of humanitarian organizations — most fiercely Muslim charities — and the vehement assault on Islam and its adherents, including their worldwide brutalization, besieging, internment, displacement, and victimization through unimaginable traumas — are not coincidental happenings. They are the calculated, synergistic processes of a complex system designed to transfer human possessions and power upward to a small cohort from the billions below. It is for this reason that its beneficiaries across the world work so hard to eliminate the sacrosanct spaces of human transactional freedom. It affords them immunity from public moral account of the means by which they usurp the wealth of the people and aggregate it to themselves, and it enables them to operate in a free stratosphere above the laws that all societies lay down to preserve their commonweal through the enforcement of just and fair financial practices.

The strategy of these digital robber barons is old and simple. Make villains of a distinct group in society by relentlessly propagating their differences of belief, ethnicity, and origin from the "normative" public, as well as the implacable incompatibility of their antiquated tradition with an evolved, cultural civility. Spread fear of them among people through mythical narratives of the violent threat they pose in society's very midst and of the secret designs they *all* harbor to suppress the nation's proud freedoms. Then panic that public by equating the victimized group with singled-out, savage events at home and in faraway lands and a still greater

162

treachery yet to be … without decisive, preemptive action.

Nothing better prepares a frightened people to trade their own freedoms for the perception of security than the nod and the wink that these new laws of tyranny — sanctioned methods of inhumanity, unapproved wars of aggression, wholesale surveillance of civil society, and the utter rejection of the inalienable right to broad, individual privacy — apply to "them" not "us." Yet if history bears out one truth, it is that once people sanction the introduction of even a limited totalitarian malignancy into their midst, its political movers and shakers (nearly synonymous in our times with the affluent) will find irresistible the power and riches this tyranny can gather to them if they but unleash it to metastasize through the length and breadth of the body politic. They may do so in premeditated stages, honing in on one group and then another, but let there be no doubt, it will consume us all. None in any lower strata of society (and we are virtually all beneath this fast-thinning upper echelon) will be saved from its ravages. Think not that democracy will save us. Despite much civic narco-babble to the contrary, majoritarian rule is no panacea against concentrated power's virulent growth.

In his 1995 Encyclical "On the Value and Inviolability of Human Life," Pope John Paul II warned exactly of this:

> Even in participatory systems of government, the regulation of interests often occurs to the advantage of the most powerful, since they are the ones most capable of maneuvering not only the levers of power but also of shaping the formation of consensus. In such a situation, democracy easily becomes an empty word.

If our societies (indeed, this human race) are to survive the new dark age of inequality and materialism run amok which we have entered upon, we must break the ever more intricate trelliswork of corruption that we have allowed the "puissant opulent" (whom the Quran dubs the *mutrifîhâ*) to build over us. And if we are to deconstruct their illusory handiwork, it is essential that we begin at their own beginning: by releasing people from the powerful spell of fear and hate that originally enchanted them, the one that has bound them to an inveterate "othering" of Muslims.

It is true that the American Indian and the African-American have borne the dehumanizing sequestration and chains of America's early fictional social saga for centuries, and the brutal beat goes on. Yet the myths and fallacies of America's most recent self-justifying iteration of select supremacy put Muslims and their religion, Islam, squarely at their center. They intentionally form the logical sequence of a malicious public program that seeks to alter the natural human embrace of justice, equality, and freedom for all that does exist at the center of the American psyche to one of inherent supremacy of some over others, of the duly deserving and undeserving, and of merited masters and the fittingly debased, which is never far from the nationalistic mindset.

These deliberately popularized, cubist mischaracterizations of Muslims and Islam form the germ of the self-destructive disease that has yielded sway in the current American mentality from the *Common Sense*, egalitarian outlook articulated in 1776 by Thomas Paine to the xenophobic, nativist blindness we witness today. Their end game is nothing higher than to elevate themselves in power and lucre, but their playbook entails weaponizing these travesties of Muslims and Islam. They understand that shifting the public mind so radically away from its higher perceptions to a place of fear from which they can manipulate it toward their grasping ends requires mythologizing an enemy of the people to justify the kinds of freedoms they will ask them to forgo and give over to them as their overlords. That is why these myth-makers have focused so obsessively on America's Muslim charities, because our human service in the urban streets of America, in its rural and coastal settings overwhelmed by natural disaster, and, yes, among the widows and orphans of war and calamity among Muslims abroad give the lie to their constant conjuring of American Muslim disloyalty, violence, and disdain for all others and threaten to undo them.

This book seeks to rally Americans to our civic covenants of liberty, our constitutional commitments to justice, our social contracts of equality, and our human disposition to compassion and charity. It exposes layers of misconception that a covetous few of selfish, ill intent have foisted on many of us to exalt themselves beyond Heaven's morality and public liability as they revel in an endless stream of ill-gotten gains while the common man and woman, and many innocent children here and across the world, are reduced to indigence down in the dust.

These pages come down to three appeals: Dispel the myths about the Muslim in our midst seeking to pay his Zakat alms to a near neighbor or bear her witness afar with a war-orphan's gift, and believe none who

164

cry "other!" The American byword has never been security at any price, but rather freedom. Restore, then, its most defining liberty: the right to believe and to act on that belief by helping another, solely for the sake of God. Reestablish and make expansive that hallowed space in which people freely transact in the real currency of their humanity. Charity.

Then can this Muslim charity, the Zakat Foundation of America, stand in its proper intervening place, becoming the prayer of the openhanded giver and the plea of the suppliant in need.